WorshipPoints

Chris Warren

WorshipPoints: A Liturgical Resource for Year C
ISBN: Softcover 978-0-692320-66-2
Copyright © 2017 by Chris Warren

All rights reserved. No part of this book may be reproduced or transmitted in any form or by any means, electronic or mechanical, including photocopying, recording, or by any information storage and retrieval system, without permission in writing from the publisher.

To order additional copies of this book, contact:

Parson's Porch Books
1-423-475-7308
www.parsonsporch.com

Parson's Porch Books is an imprint of **Parson's Porch & Book Publishers** in Cleveland, Tennessee, which has double focus. We focus on the needs of creative writers who need a professional publisher to get their work to market, **&** we also focus on the needs of others by sharing our profits with those who struggle in poverty to meet their basic needs of food, clothing, shelter and safety.

WorshipPoints

Contents

First Sunday of Advent 9
Second Sunday of Advent 11
Third Sunday of Advent 13
Fourth Sunday of Advent 15
Nativity of the Lord 17
First Sunday After Christmas 19
Epiphany 21
Second Sunday after Christmas Day 23
Second Sunday of Epiphany 25
Second Sunday after Epiphany 27
Third Sunday after the Epiphany 29
Fourth Sunday after the Epiphany 31
Transfiguration Sunday 33
Fifth Sunday after the Epiphany 35
Sixth Sunday after the Epiphany 37
Seventh Sunday after the Epiphany 39
Eighth Sunday after the Epiphany 41
Ninth Sunday after the Epiphany 43
Ash Wednesday 45
First Sunday of Lent 47
Second Sunday of Lent 49
Third Sunday of Lent 51
Fourth Sunday of Lent 53
Fifth Sunday of Lent 55
Liturgy of the Palms 57
Liturgy of the Passion 59
Resurrection of the Lord 61

Resurrection of the Lord (Alternative)	63
Second Sunday of Easter	65
Third Sunday of Easter	67
Fourth Sunday of Easter	69
Fifth Sunday of Easter	71
Sixth Sunday of Easter	73
Seventh Sunday of Easter	75
Ascension of the Lord	77
Day of Pentecost	79
Trinity Sunday (First Sunday after Pentecost)	81
Proper 3	83
Proper 4	85
Proper 5	87
Proper 6	89
Proper 7	91
Proper 8	93
Proper 9	95
Proper 10	97
Proper 11	99
Proper 12	101
Proper 13	103
Proper 14	105
Proper 15	107
Proper 16	109
Proper 17	111
Proper 18	113
Proper 19	115
Proper 20	117
Proper 21	119

Proper 22	121
Proper 23	123
Proper 24	125
Proper 25	127
Proper 26	129
Proper 27	131
Proper 28	133
Proper 29 Reign of Christ	135
All Saints Day	137

First Sunday of Advent

Scripture
Jeremiah 33:14-16
Psalm 25:1-10
1 Thessalonians 3:9-13
Luke 21:25-36

Call to Worship
One: To you, O Lord, we lift up our souls.
O God, in you we trust.
Many: Make your ways known to us, O God.
Teach us your paths.
One: Lead us in your truth and teach us.
Do not let us be put to shame.
Many: You are the God of our salvation.
For you, we wait expectantly.
One: Do not remember our sins and transgressions.
Remember us in goodness, according to your steadfast love.
Many: The Lord is good and upright!
We praise you with all we have.

Invocation
Lord God, our salvation, in your name we gather for worship, and through your grace we rejoice in the wonder of your many gifts to us. Reveal to us in this hour new visions of yourself and help us to worship you in truth and love. Your paths are steadfast love and faithfulness. Cause us to be willingly led by you on those paths. Amen.

Call to Confession
The psalmist cries out to God, "Do not remember the sins of my youth or my transgressions; according to your steadfast love remember me, for your goodness' sake, O Lord!" None can stand before God trusting in our own righteousness, but all must confess their misdeeds before God that we might be forgiven. Let us pray.

Unison Prayer of Confession
Lord of all, be mindful of your mercy. Remember your people. We bow before you now calling to mind our sins against one another and against you. We trust in your mercy and forgiveness to rescue us from our bondage to sin. Please forgive us and keep us on your paths.

Assurance of Forgiveness
The Lord leads the humble in what is right. The Lord teaches the humble God's way. We are forgiven when we turn from the sinful ways we have embraced and repent of those ways. Thanks be to God for this great mercy!

Offertory Invitation
How can we thank God enough for all the joy we have received? How can we return thanks to God for the gifts that we have accepted? We cannot return to God in equal measure, but we can give of our time, our talents, and our treasures that others may know the joy we have received in Christ. Our offerings are one way we begin to do this.

Offertory Prayer
Wonderful, loving God, our offerings are nothing compared to the great and awesome gifts you have given to us. We ask that you receive them and that you would use them to bring your good news to others in this world. We pray that you would make us more willing to give of ourselves. Amen.

Benediction
The kingdom of God is near. May the Lord make us to increase and abound in love for one another, and may the Lord so strengthen our hearts in holiness that we may be blameless before our God at the coming of the Lord Jesus Christ.

Second Sunday of Advent

Scripture
Malachi 3:1-4
Luke 1:68-79
Philippians 1:3-11
Luke 3:1-6

Call to Worship
One: Blessed be the Lord God of Israel, who has looked favorably on the people.
God has redeemed us by raising up a mighty savior from David's house.
Many: God told of this savior through the prophets of old.
Through him, we are saved from our enemies and shown great mercy.
One: Through God's promise, we can serve God without fear,
In holiness and righteousness all our days.
Many: The gift of the savior is without equal in all the world.
Praise God for the wonder of our salvation.
One: Just as John was called to proclaim the word of the Lord,
So God has called us, to prepare Christ's way in our land.
Many: May we be messengers of great joy to all people.
May we bring good news to all we encounter!

Invocation
We call upon you, the Lord, the designer of the cosmos, to come and be with us as we worship. We affirm your presence with us wherever we are, and we call upon your Spirit, O Lord to enlighten, to uplift, and to grant new wisdom and insight to us during this time of praise. May the great three in one move among us today that we will be made new by encountering God.

Call to Confession
John was called to be a witness to the light of Christ to the world. The church is called to perform the same work. Yet we have not always been focused on this as our work in the world. We have become subject to too many distractions that divert us from the work of preparing Christ's way. Let us confess those shortcomings before God.

Prayer of Confession
We have placed ourselves and worldly things above you, O great God. We have sometimes lost sight of the importance of our witness in the world, and we have neglected to offer you true worship. We have allowed other

interests to creep into our lives between you and ourselves. We humbly confess our sinfulness and ask that you would help us to reorder our lives around your will for the world.

Assurance of Forgiveness
As we celebrate the gift of the Christ to the world, we remember the words of John's gospel that God did not send the son into the world to condemn the world, but that the world might be saved through him. It is God's will that humans be saved. We take great comfort in this, knowing that we have hope of salvation through the Christ.

Offertory Invitation
Our calling to prepare the way of Christ into the world is one that we should fulfill with all we have and all we are. One way to prepare Christ's entrance is through giving to the ministries of the church that the church may be better able to provide hope for the hopeless, food for the hungry, release to the captive, and good news to all people. Let us give generously.

Offertory Prayer
Ruler of all, we offer our very selves to you. We give you our hearts, our lives, and our treasures. Please bless these gifts that they may reach to places we could never have imagined. We pray that all our gifts may be used to reach out in love to your world. Amen.

Benediction
Thanks to God for the gifts of the Spirit that are present here in this congregation. May we continue to share the gospel with the world in great joy, in gratitude for the wonderful gift of our Savior, Jesus the Christ. Amen.

Third Sunday of Advent

Scripture
Zephaniah 3:14-20
Isaiah 12:2-6
Philippians 4:4-7
Luke 3:7-18

Call to Worship
One: Surely God is our Salvation!
We will trust in the Lord and not be afraid.
Many: The LORD God is our strength and our might.
God has become our salvation!
One: With great joy we will draw from the waters of salvation.
And we will say together in that day:
Many: Give thanks to the LORD, Call on God's name.
Make God's deeds known throughout the world and exalt God's name!
One: Sing praises to the LORD, for God has done gloriously.
Let this be known throughout the entire earth.
Many: Shout aloud and sing for joy, all people,
For great in our midst is the Holy One.

Invocation
Lord, you are in our midst, giving victory over adversity. We rejoice that you are with us and we worship you in truthfulness and sincerity. God of truth and righteousness renew us in this time of worship. We pray that you would bring all humankind into loving relationship with God and with one another.

Call to Confession
John called those who gathered for baptism a "brood of vipers." He was describing people who proclaimed they followed God but were far from God in their hearts. We strive to be people who follow God in truth and righteousness, but we realize that sometimes John's description may also be appropriate for us. Let us confess our sins.

Prayer of Confession
Lord God, giver of grace, forgive our lack of devotion to you. As individuals and as a people we have allowed ourselves to be taken in by the world. We have lost sight of your love for humanity and our need to devote ourselves to you and to love of our neighbors. Forgive us, we pray, and lead us forward in the light of your love.

Assurance of Forgiveness
God has become our salvation. Through the gift we celebrate this season God has reached into the world proclaiming love for us and forgiveness for all who turn from their sin and give themselves again unto God. Thanks be to God for this great and wonderful gift!

Offertory Invitation
Realizing that we have sometimes been uncommitted to the things God has called us to, we turn our hearts to full giving unto God. We hold nothing back, giving that the good news of Christ may reach all, the world over. Let us give generously.

Offertory Prayer
Wonderful Ruler of the nations, as a people we return these gifts to you. They are only tokens, but may they be tokens of faithfulness, used by this congregation to bring healing to this area and the world. Help us to remember that gifts of all we have, not simply our money, are required. Amen.

Benediction
Rejoice in the Lord always! Again, I say, Rejoice!
Let your gentleness be known to everyone. The Lord is near.
Go with God to love and serve all creation.
Amen.

Fourth Sunday of Advent

Scripture
Micah 5:2-5a
Luke 1:46b-55 or Psalm 80:1-7
Hebrews 10:5-10
Luke 1:39-45 (46-55)

Call to Worship
One: God is sending the one who is to rule.
The one whose origin is from of old, from ancient days.
Many: The one to come will be a shepherd to the people.
This one will lead the flock in righteousness.
One: In the strength of the LORD shall the messiah stand,
In the majesty of the LORD our God.
Many: The people shall live in security.
God's name shall be made great even to the ends of the earth.
One: The coming ruler shall bring peace to the earth.
The new creation of the LORD shall last forever.
Many: God of all, send your messiah here.
Send the messiah that this world may know your peace.

Invocation
Out of Bethlehem comes the one who is to reign forever and ever. From the most humble of beginnings will come the messiah of the entire world. We thank you, God, for this gift to the world even as we look forward to the celebration of Christmas day. May your spirit, the Spirit of Christ, inspire us all to give our lives to the ruler of all nations.

Call to Confession
Even as we worship the one and only God, we are reminded of the ways that we have been unable to fulfill our promises and obligations to you. We have sinned against you and against our fellow humans. Our focus has been on things that do not please you. Move in us that we may sincerely repent before you.

Prayer of Confession
Give ear to your people, O great shepherd of the universe. We have had our minds on things that are not of you. We have made choices that do not please you or bring us closer to you. We have forgotten our promises and have gone our own way. Bring us back together in your true and full fellowship. Forgive and lead us in your better way.

Assurance of Forgiveness
Once and for all the sacrifice has been made for all people. The birth, life, death, and resurrection of the Christ has given atonement to all people. We who come to God repenting of our sins are accepted, forgiven and redeemed. Thanks to God for this wonderful promise.

Offertory Invitation
Even as Christ was willing to come from glory to serve the people of this world, we, too, must set aside our attempts to gain glory and give of ourselves to serve others the world over. We give all we can, that the love of Christ might reach to all people on earth. May the blessings of Christ that we celebrate this season be spread through our offerings to God in this worship time and at all times.

Offertory Prayer
Your gift of love to the world is greater than any gift we could ever return to you, Lord God. We offer these gifts that we have this day unto you, asking for your blessing and praying that they may be used to achieve your purposes through the community gathered here. Help us to be willing to use all we have to glorify you. Amen.

Benediction
The Christ is coming! His presence in our hearts will change us and through us, the world will be changed. May we heartily accept this gift and give of it that we may continually prepare the way of the Lord. Amen.

Nativity of the Lord

Scripture
Isaiah 52:7-10
Psalm 98
Hebrews 1:1-4 (5-12)
John 1:1-14

Call to Worship
One: In the beginning was the Word,
and the Word was with God, and the Word was God.
Many: All things came into being through him.
Without him, not one thing came into being.
One: In him was life,
And the life was the light of all people.
Many: The light shines in the darkness.
The darkness did not overcome it.
One: The true light that enlightens all
Is coming into the world.
Many: To all who receive him,
Power is given to become children of God.

Invocation
Your Word has become flesh, Holy One. Your very self has come into the world as a human child. Just like all of us, you were born a helpless and tiny baby. Just like us you lived and breathed and ate and did all the things humans have done from the beginning of time. Come to us again in this hour of worship. Meet us here and cause us to recognize you as our God and as our sibling.

Call to Confession
The Word became flesh and came among the people. The people did not recognize the Word, because they were not acquainted with the Light of the world. The people living today are also strangers to the light. We have wandered far away. Let us confess our sinfulness.

Prayer of Confession
Lord God, you created us. You made us to be a holy and loving people. We have lost our way. We have not loved, we have not given ourselves to you, and we have not forgiven one another. We have not lived as you commanded. Forgive us and cause us to walk forward in the light.

Assurance of Forgiveness
John testified to the Light. Christ came for people everywhere. Christ came for us. And Christ came that, even though we were not walking in the light, we might find the light through him. As we repent of our sins and turn ourselves toward the light, we are promised forgiveness. Thanks be to God!

Offertory Invitation
God has done marvelous things. Salvation has been revealed in the sight of all nations. The God we worship is a wonderful, loving, giving God. Let us give back to God of our riches, of our time and talents. Let us give of our very selves.

Offertory Prayer
Receive these gifts, Gracious God, and help us to withhold nothing from you. Use these gifts through us, your servants, and through every means possible, to show the Light of the world to more and more people. We pray that we may be a part of the revealing of your Son to the world. Amen.

Benediction
How beautiful are the feet of those who bring the good news to the nations!
Go now and take the news. Salvation has come!
Praise to God, in Christ, through the Holy Spirit!

First Sunday After Christmas

Scripture
1 Samuel 2:18-20, 26
Psalm 148
Colossians 3:12-17
Luke 2:41-52

Call to Worship
One: Praise the LORD!
Praise the LORD from the heavens, praise the LORD in the heights!
Many: Praise God, all angels; praise God, all hosts!
Praise God, sun and moon and shining stars!
One: Let all things praise the name of the LORD,
For God commanded, and they were created.
Many: God established creation in a time beyond human knowledge.
God set the boundaries of all creation, boundaries that may not be passed.
One: Let us all praise the name of the LORD,
For God's name alone is to be exalted.
Many: God's glory is above the heavens and the earth!
Let us praise the LORD!

Invocation
Maker of all, we praise you as the creator of all things. You have given life and breath and all the things that we need to be sustained. You continue to bless us with love and grace and many, many more gifts. We worship you this day, and we invoke your Spirit to come upon us. Draw us closer to you that we may be the disciples you have called us to be. Amen.

Call to Confession
We are called to be clothed in compassion, kindness, humility, meekness, and patience. We are called to be a loving and forgiving people. But, since we are people, we are imperfect in these things. Truly we have neglected to be compassionate, kind, humble, meek, and patient. Truly we have been unloving and unforgiving. We call those times to mind as we pray before God for forgiveness.

Prayer of Confession
Great and Gracious God, we have been unable to follow the way you have set for us. We have been unable to love. We have refused to forgive. We have hurt one another and ourselves in our inability to follow your call on our lives. Help us to see where our society and we as individuals have fallen short of your will for us. Forgive us and cause us to truly repent.

Assurance of Forgiveness
The love of Christ rules in the hearts of those who know Christ as their savior. The blessings of Christ are vast, and they include forgiveness for those who confess of their sins and repent of their sinfulness. Christ meets us here and desires forgiveness for us as a community and for each member of the community. Humbly repent, and you are forgiven.

Offertory Invitation
The LORD desires and deserves our full commitment. We know God as the creator of all things, as one who loves humanity, and as one who has sent a redeemer to help us, that we may have salvation. To this God we give our gifts this day. May they be generous.

Offertory Prayer
Mighty God, our gifts have been collected and we place them in your hands. May we have the wisdom to use them in ways that please you. May we have the strength to give more than we think we can afford. May we worship you through the giving back of all we have been given. Amen.

Benediction
May the peace of Christ rule in all our hearts, as we were all called into one body. Let us be thankful and let the word of Christ dwell within us richly. Whatever we do, in word or deed, may we do everything in the name of the Lord Jesus, giving thanks to God through him. Amen.

Epiphany

Scripture
Isaiah 60:1-6
Psalm 72:1-7, 10-14
Ephesians 3:1-12
Matthew 2:1-12

Call to Worship
One: Arise, shine; for your light has come!
The glory of the LORD has risen upon you!
Many: The glory of the LORD shall be known to all.
The light shall shine for all to see.
One: Although darkness shall cover the earth,
Thick darkness shall cover the people,
Many: The LORD will arise upon the people,
and God's glory will appear over us.
One: Nations come to bring their wealth.
They bring their wonders to give to the LORD.
Many: They shall bring gold and frankincense,
They shall proclaim the praise of the LORD.

Invocation
Draw all people to yourself, Loving God. May your desires be the desires of your people. Help us to recognize you in all the world, within the church, and far away from the influence of the church. Meet us here in this place and claim us as your own. Amen.

Call to Confession
The psalmist declares that the LORD delivers the needy when they call. The LORD has pity on the weak and poor. The LORD redeems those who live in violence and oppression. These are the desires of the LORD. How close have our hearts been to these desires?

Prayer of Confession
Great One, when we remember your promises to the poor and needy, when we think of your desire to rescue those in oppression and amidst violence, we realize that we have focused so much on ourselves we cannot always even see those needs. Forgive us and help us to use your love to do your work in this world.

Assurance of Forgiveness
In our humility, God hears our plea for forgiveness. In our repentance, God will forgive our inability to be all we have been asked to be. When we humbly repent, we are forgiven. Praise God for this promise!

Offertory Invitation
Kings from far away traveled great distances to give gifts to the Christ child. They gave gifts of great value to the young king. Our gifts are also offered to Christ and they, too, should be of the best that we have. Let us give all we can.

Offertory Prayer
Christ take these gifts and use them to fulfill your purposes. We dedicate them to you and pray that they may heal people in our area and throughout the world. Since you have loved so much, please use these gifts to spread that love to all we can reach.

Benediction

As we continue to follow the star of Jesus, know that Christ can make all things new.
As we leave this sanctuary, take Christ's love to all you meet.

Second Sunday after Christmas Day

Scripture
Jeremiah 31:7-14
Psalm 147:12-20
Ephesians 1:3-14
John 1:(1-9), 10-18

Call to Worship
One: The Word has come!
Thanks be to God!
Many: The very Word of God has come among us.
We welcome the Christ into the world.
One: The LORD is bringing all the people together.
God will gather all God's people from far away.
Many: They shall come together and sing praises.
They will eat and have their fill.
One: Peace shall reign over all the people.
The people of the LORD will be redeemed.
Many: Thanks to God for this great and glorious gift.
Thanks to God for the redemption of creation.

Invocation
Lord God, you have sent the Word into the world. Before you even sent the Christ, you knew what it would do for us, and you also knew what the cost would be. We are overwhelmed when we realize this wonderful thing done for us. May Christ's spirit be with us here, that we may learn of him. May Christ's will become our will. Help us to give back the love and praise you require. Amen.

Call to Confession
We have been called as adopted children of the most high God. Even though we live in this call, we have not been able to follow God's laws and desires perfectly. We have sinned against God and against our fellow humans. Let us humbly confess and repent.

Prayer of Confession
We confess, awesome God, that, even though we call ourselves your people, we have stumbled along the way. We have forgotten to give you your due. Our hearts have been far from you and your people. Instead, we have focused on ourselves and our worldly desires. Forgive us, we pray, and help us to be made new in your love.

Assurance of Forgiveness
Through Christ we have redemption. We have the forgiveness of our trespasses according to Christ's grace. We have been adopted as children of the most high God and through Christ have been redeemed. Let us rejoice!

Offertory Invitation
God has lavished upon us grace after grace, blessing after blessing. As part of our worship, we turn our minds to what we can give back to God. Through our offering, we are to give our very best back to God gratefully thanking God for all we have received.

Offertory Prayer
We dedicate our gifts and ourselves to Christ in this time of worship. We pray that you would shower the people with blessings through the worshipers gathered here and through the gifts we have returned to you. May the world see love through us. Amen.

Benediction
Blessed be the God and Father of the Lord Jesus Christ!
God has blessed us all in Christ with every spiritual blessing in the heavenly places.
Let us live our lives in response to that love.

Second Sunday of Epiphany

Baptism of the Lord

Scripture
Isaiah 43:1-7
Psalm 29
Acts 8:14-17
Luke 3:15-17, 21-22

Call to Worship
One: Thus says the LORD, who created you,
Do not fear.
Many: For I have redeemed you.
I have called you by name; you are mine.
One: When you pass through the waters,
When you walk through fire,
Many: The waters will not overwhelm you.
The flames will not consume you.
One: I will be with you, says the LORD.
You are precious in my sight; I love you.
Many: Do not fear, for I am with you.
Everyone, whom I formed and made.

Invocation
On this day that we remember the baptism of the Lord Jesus, cause us to remember our baptisms as well, Great One. You are our source, you are our savior. Through our baptisms, we were sealed in the Holy Spirit. Send your Spirit once again. Renew our excitement in our relationship with you, this day, this hour. Amen.

Call to Confession
The people of this age are just like those who came to be baptized by John. We need to be reminded that Christ's winnowing fork is in his hand. He comes both to judge and to forgive. At this time, we remember our sins so that through confession, we can receive Christ's forgiveness.

Prayer of Confession
In our baptism, LORD God, you claimed us as your own. Yet we have gone our own way. We have participated in the things of this world. We have forgotten you and we have been consumed by the fires of our earthly wants. Hear us as we confess our sins, and forgive us, we pray.

Assurance of Forgiveness
Just as God promised to be with God's people in the deep waters and in the fires, God remains with us even when we do not follow God's path. God chooses to forgive when we ask, when we truly recognize our sinfulness and turn again to God. Be certain God's promise is for all of us.

Offertory Invitation
We, who have received the Holy Spirit, out of gratitude for all we have, give ourselves and our gifts back to God. We give lovingly, not grudgingly. We give gratefully, not out of obligation. We give generously and faithfully.

Offertory Prayer
All we have and all we are we offer to you this day. Use these gifts we have given and use all the things we have and are for your glory here in the world. We love you and we pray for your will to be done on earth and your kingdom to come. May our gifts help to bring your Spirit to all the earth.

Benediction
May the LORD strengthen us all, that, as we remember our baptisms, we can more fully incorporate the Spirit of God and the love of Christ into all we say, all we do, all we are. Let us go now to serve the God of all!

Second Sunday after Epiphany

Scripture
Isaiah 62:1-5
Psalm 36:5-10
1 Corinthians 12:1-11
John 2:1-11

Call to Worship
One: The love of the LORD is steadfast;
It extends to the heavens.
Many: God's faithfulness reaches to the clouds.
God's righteousness is like the mighty mountain.
One: The judgments of the LORD are like the great deep.
The LORD saves humans and animals alike.
Many: O God, your steadfast love is precious!
All people may take refuge in the shadow of your wings!
One: We feast on the abundance of the LORD's house.
We drink from the river of God's delights.
Many: With you, O God is the fountain of life;
In your light, we see light.

Invocation
Mighty one, may we know your steadfast love, and may we receive your salvation. You have called your people to be a crown of beauty, a royal diadem in your hand. We strive to be what you have called us to be. Help us to find you this day. Help us to invite your Spirit in. Cause us to commit ourselves to you.

Call to Confession
We have received good gifts from God's hand, but we have often chosen to pursue other goals. We know that God has given us all gifts to use for the uplifting of the kinship God desires, but we have not practiced their use, and we have chosen to try to develop gifts that benefit our greed rather than God's will. Let us confess before the Lord of all.

Prayer of Confession
Forgiving and loving maker, we have gone our own way. As groups and as individuals we have tried to change your gifts for us. We have sometimes intended to walk in your way but lost our path, and we have sometimes purposefully chosen to do things contrary to what we understand your will to be. Show us our real gifts, our real way, and give us the commitment to follow.

Assurance of Forgiveness
God's salvation has already reached to the ends of the earth. The work of Jesus the Christ was for all people and is available to all people. When we recognize our sins, we are expected to confess them and then turn from them. We have faith that in doing so, we are healed.

Offertory Invitation
Our God is a God of amazing and miraculous wonders. So many blessings flow to the people of this world, and so many blessings have come to each of us in this worship space. One faithful response to those blessings is a generous gift of our treasures for God's use in the world. We offer our wealth and ourselves in this time.

Offertory Prayer
Giver of life, we offer these gifts to you. May we be serious when we offer our hearts and our lives as well. Bring others into the light that you shine through our monetary gifts and through the gift we have been given to love humanity in the name of Christ. Amen.

Benediction
There are as many gifts in this space as there are people. In fact, since many are given multiple gifts, there are many more than the number of those present. Let us go forth this day, offering those gifts to the Sovereign God from whom they have been given. Amen.

Third Sunday after the Epiphany

Scripture
Nehemiah 8:1-3, 5-6, 8-10
Psalm 19
1 Corinthians 12:12-31a
Luke 4:14-21

Call to Worship
One: The heavens are telling the glory of God;
The firmament proclaims God's handiwork.
Many: Creation tells of God's wonder and majesty.
Day and night, it declares the knowledge of the LORD.
One: The law of the LORD is perfect, reviving the soul.
The decrees of the LORD are sure, making even the simplest wise.
Many: God's ways are more to be desired than gold, even much fine gold.
God's ways are sweeter than honey and drippings of the honeycomb.
One: Show your people your ways, mighty God.
Cause us to understand your will.
Many: May the words of our mouths and the meditations of our hearts
be acceptable to you, O LORD, our rock and our redeemer.

Invocation
Stir within us during these moments of prayer and praise, LORD God, holy one. Break through the walls that we erect to separate ourselves from you. Burst into our lives and fill us with the fire of pure devotion to your ways. Make us new and make us only yours. Amen.

Call to Confession
The psalmist writes, "But who can detect their errors? Clear from me hidden faults." We who study the laws of God still are unable to fully know our own transgressions. Let us call to mind those things of which we are aware and pray for illumination and forgiveness of those sins of which we do not even know.

Prayer of Confession
Gracious one, we truly do not know all the ways we have sinned against you, against your people, and against your perfect way for us. We have ignored the suffering in your world. We have worked tirelessly for our own gain, ignoring the least among us. Help us to recognize our sinfulness and help us to overcome it.

Assurance of Forgiveness
Jesus was the fulfillment of the prophecies that released the captives, restored sight to the blind, brought good news to the poor, and let the oppressed go free. Jesus came that those who were in sin may be saved. In the grace of Jesus, we are forgiven.

Offertory Invitation
Our spiritual gifts are many and different. What we have was given to us to be used for the kinship of God's people and for the increase of God's kingdom on earth. Let us dedicate our lives and our gifts to God's purposes for creation.

Offertory Prayer
Lord, we offer to you that which you have given to us. May our hearts yearn to praise you through our gifts. May our spirits desire the same things you desire in your world. May our hearts break for the ways people are hurt, oppressed, and downtrodden, and may we use all we have and all we are to care for these.

Benediction
You are the body of Christ, and you are each individually members of it. If one member suffers, all suffer along with it, and if one member is honored, all members are honored along with it.
Let us go, striving for greater gifts, that we may live as one body united for the love of Christ.
Amen.

Fourth Sunday after the Epiphany

Scripture
Jeremiah 1:4-10
Psalm 71:1-6
1 Corinthians 13:1-13
Luke 4:21-30

Call to Worship
One: In you, O LORD, I take refuge.
Let me never be put to shame.
Many: In your righteousness deliver me and rescue me.
Incline your ear to me and save me.
One: Be to me a rock of refuge, a strong fortress.
Save me, O LORD, for you are my rock and my fortress.
Many: Though the world opposes me, though I grow faint,
You, O LORD, are my shield and my strength.
One: All grow weary, all find their own strength will fail,
But the strength of the LORD sustains God's people.
Many: Let us lean on you and learn from you,
Let us continually praise God's name.

Invocation
LORD, God, you are a God of love. You have taught us that out of the wonderful attributes of faith, hope, and love, the greatest of all these is love. Help us to be creatures of love. Help us to know your love, to show your love, and to give your love to each other, to all your people, and to you. Re-make us in your image of love today. Amen.

Call to Confession
Our lives are uncertain, and our commitments are unsure. We are called to be a loving, forgiving, and holy people, but we have not fully fulfilled that call. Where we have made mistakes or consciously acted against the way in which God has called us, we have sinned. Let us confess before God our faults that we may be healed.

Prayer of Confession
Holy and Awesome God, we confess that we have been unable to completely set aside our human ways to walk in your light. We have not known the way of love as you have commanded us. We have neglected things you have asked us to do, and we have done things that dishonor you. Forgive us for our lack of love and heal us.

Assurance of Forgiveness
The God of love has shown perfect love to humanity and to individuals. We can never be the perfect people we desire to be, yet God loves and forgives and heals us when we turn to God in humble repentance. Thank you, Great One, for your unfailing love.

Offertory Invitation
Everything we have, own, and are we owe to God. When we worship in our time of offering, God expects us to give ourselves back to God. Give abundantly, that the way of love may extend to the ends of the earth.

Offertory Prayer
Use these gifts, Wonderful God, for the healing of your people and for the increase of the brightness of your light in the world. May all who see us and know us recognize your spirit within us, as we use all we have for you. Amen.

Benediction
Now we see in a mirror, dimly.
Then we will see face to face.
Now we know only in part;
Then we will know fully, even as we are fully known.
Go and share God's love in all you say and do.
Amen.

Transfiguration Sunday

Scripture
Exodus 34:29-35
Psalm 99
2 Corinthians 3:12-4:2
Luke 9:28-36, (37-43a)

Call to Worship
One: The LORD, our God is king! Let the peoples tremble!
God sits enthroned upon the cherubim; let the earth quake!
Many: The LORD is great in Zion; God is exalted over all people.
Let us praise God's great and awesome name. Holy is the LORD!
One: The mighty king and lover of justice has established equity.
God has executed justice and righteousness among God's people.
Many: Extol the LORD, our God. Worship at God's footstool.
Holy is the LORD!
One: The LORD hears those who cry out to God.
God is forgiving and answers the people of the covenant.
Many: Extol the Lord our God, and worship at the holy mountain.
The LORD, our God, is holy!

Invocation
LORD above all creation, you are holy indeed– far holier than we humans can imagine or fathom. As we worship in your sanctuary this day, help us to recognize this place as a place where you dwell. Let us set aside the things that occupy our minds and take our resources and help us to focus all we have and are on you. May our worship of you be true and all encompassing. Amen.

Call to Confession
We often hear the words of God or see the things of God and they appear to us as if we have placed a veil over our faces, so that those words are muffled, and the visions are unclear. We have purposefully separated ourselves from the path God has set before us. Let us confess before our God.

Prayer of Confession
LORD be to us a God of grace in this time. We have placed barriers between ourselves and you. We have tried to be distant from you and your law. We have found ways to reason that what we are doing is not sinful at all. Reveal to us our sinfulness. Let us recognize it that we may repent and be forgiven.

Assurance of Forgiveness
Where the Spirit of the Lord is, there is freedom. We who worship the God of love are free to call upon that God for mercy and for grace when we recognize our faults, ask for forgiveness, and turn away from our sins. The Lord is faithful to forgive.

Offertory Invitation
Take a moment to realize just how blessed we are as a congregation and as individuals. We take for granted things that many in this world could hardly dream of. Knowing how God has commanded us to care for the poor, knowing how Christ lived out that command, and being empowered by God's Holy Spirit, let us give of ourselves in this time of offering.

Offertory Prayer
Please accept our gifts, God of mercy. Reveal to us how you would have us use all our gifts so that we may faithfully serve you as your children. Grant that we may have the faith to give more, so that your world may be blessed through us. Amen.

Benediction
May we be like those who saw Jesus heal the young boy,
Astounded now and always by the greatness of God.
May God's love, Christ's grace, and the sustaining power
of God's Holy Spirit be with you all wherever you may go.
Amen.

Fifth Sunday after the Epiphany

Scripture
Isaiah 6:1-8 (9-13)
Psalm 138
1 Corinthians 15:1-11
Luke 5:1-11

Call to Worship
One: The angels in the presence of God sing unceasingly.
They sing a song of beauty and of great praise:
Many: "Holy, holy, holy is the LORD of hosts!
The whole earth is full of God's glory!"
One: The LORD looks out into the world and says,
"Whom shall I send? Who will go for me?"
Many: We the faithful of the LORD respond,
"Here we are! Send us!"
One: Let all give thanks to the God of all
Let us thank God for the call to serve.
Many: May we become servants in your name, mighty God!
Send us that we may do your work in the world!

Invocation
Lord, you are mighty beyond measure. You are great and awesome and high above the things of this earth. Yet, you regard us. You remember us, you care for us, you save us. Help us to know your love, help us to see your workings in the world and in ourselves, help us to love so that we respond faithfully to all you have done for your people. Amen.

Call to Confession
We were called to love. But, like Paul we have persecuted others. In overt and subtle ways, we have placed ourselves first in our quest for more. We have allowed others to go uncared for and unloved. Let us confess our sins before God.

Prayer of Confession
Great One, we cannot even clearly see all our sinfulness. We know of some of our misdeeds. We know of some ways we have strayed from you. We ask that you continue to show us how we have done poorly and how we can do better. Forgive us our evil ways and lead us in your way.

Assurance of Forgiveness
By the grace of God, we are what we are. We cannot become children of God by doing great and marvelous deeds. We can only receive salvation through the grace given to us by Jesus. When we call on his name and recognize our sins, striving to do better, Jesus is faithful to forgive.

Offertory Invitation
Our nets are full almost to bursting. Even if we do not have riches to speak of, we have the blessings of ourselves and our gifts. All of these can and should be given back to God. Let us give to God all we have received.

Offertory Prayer
We offer all these sacrifices to you, Christ our Lord. May they heal the sick. May they feed the hungry. May they clothe the naked and give release to those who are oppressed. May they be a blessing to your people in your world. Amen.

Benediction
This is of first importance: Christ died for our sins in accordance with the **Scripture**s. He was buried, and he was raised on the third day in accordance with the **Scripture**s. He appeared to many and continues to act in the world today. Let us live lives that show that the Church is Christ's body, acting in love for the sake of the world. Amen.

Sixth Sunday after the Epiphany

Scripture
Jeremiah 17:5-10
Psalm 1
1 Corinthians 15:12-20
Luke 6:17-26

Call to Worship
One: Blessings are on the ones who follow the LORD's path;
Happy are those who do not heed the wicked.
Many: Their delight is in the law of the LORD.
They are like trees planted by streams of water.
One: They yield their fruit in its season and their leaves do not wither.
They prosper in all they do.
Many: Blessed are those who trust in the LORD,
Whose trust is in the LORD of all.
One: The LORD tests the mind and the heart.
God judges the fruit of our ways.
Many: The LORD watches over God's people.
Thanks be to GOD!

Invocation
Mighty Ruler, we proclaim our faith in you. We come this day to offer you the sacrifice of our praise. May we worship you in mind, body, and spirit. We ask that we may meet your Spirit here, that you would move within and among us that we might have great changes of heart that cause us to be better servants and to do your will. Meet us, fill us, renew us. Amen.

Call to Confession
The Psalmist writes that the wicked cannot stand before the judgment of God. We hope to be the righteous, but we recognize ways that we gone down wicked paths. Let us confess those sins before God that we may receive the grace God offers.

Prayer of Confession
Lord of all creation, our vision is cloudy. Our will is weak. Our capacity to love is poor. Our ability to understand your message for your people is imperfect. We now call to mind ways that we have participated in the wickedness of this world. Forgive us, cleanse us, and lead us from this place renewed in our devotion to you.

Assurance of Forgiveness
If Christ was not raised from the dead and if Christ had not atoned for our sins, we would indeed be a people worthy of pity. We would be without hope. But, since Christ was indeed raised from the dead as the first fruits of those who have died, we have more than hope, we have **Assurance of Forgiveness**. Thanks be to God!

Offertory Invitation
Jesus blessed the poor and spoke of woe to the rich. His message to those who had extra was to give so that all could have enough. An important part of our worship this day and every time we come together is the sacrifice of some of what we have for the good of others. Let us give that the Church may be a greater blessing.

Offertory Prayer
Accept us as we are, wonderful Savior. Accept our offerings. Take them and use them and cause them to be blessings to those near and far who are in need. We love you, Lord, and we pray that we may be a part of the spreading of your love and your mercy to your world. Amen.

Benediction
Christ has been raised from the dead,
The first fruits of those that sleep.
In Christ we, too, have new life.
Let us share that life with one another and with a world in need. Amen.

Seventh Sunday after the Epiphany

Scripture
Genesis 45:3-11, 15
Psalm 37:1-11, 39-40
1 Corinthians 15:35-38
Luke 6:27-38

Call to Worship
One: As we come into worship today,
Let us remember together the words from Jesus' great sermon.
Many: Love your enemies, do good to those who hate you.
Bless those who curse you, pray for those who abuse you.
One: If anyone strikes you on the cheek, offer the other also.
If someone takes your coat, give also your shirt.
Many: Give to all who beg from you.
If someone takes goods from you, do not ask for them again.
One: Do unto others as you would have them do unto you.
Love your enemies, do good, lend without expectation of return.
Many: Do not judge, and you will not be judged.
Do not condemn, and you will not be condemned
Forgive, and you will be forgiven.
Give, and it will be given to you.

Invocation
We hear your words, words calling us to righteous and Godly living, and we realize just how hard that is. We come in worship to encounter you, to be changed by you, to be given the power and ability to live in the way you have called and intended. Meet us here, convict us here, that we may become new creations.

Call to Confession
Have we loved our enemies? Have we blessed those who curse us? Have we judged? Have we condemned? Have we lived lives worthy of the calling that we have been given, or have we looked to our own way? We have much to confess.

Prayer of Confession
Gracious One, we often find ourselves unable to live up to the calling we profess when we take up our crosses to follow you. Help us to see those we have forgotten, or judged, or stepped on in our selfish ways. Forgive us and help us to repent and do all we can to make our human relationships and our relationship with you what it should be.

Assurance of Forgiveness
Christ, who was raised from the dead, sent a life-giving Spirit that we might also inherit the eternal kingdom of God. We are imperfect, this is true, but in our desire to be forgiven and in our forgiving of others, we have the assurance of our own forgiveness. Let us practice forgiveness that we might receive forgiveness.

Offertory Invitation
What greater measure of our love for others is there than our willingness to give of ourselves to help those in need? There are many in physical, emotional, and spiritual need in our world. We dedicate ourselves during this time of worship to heal them as we are able. Let us give all we can.

Offertory Prayer
In our offering, we dedicate not only our riches, but our very selves to you, O God. Use us. Heal others through us. Give healing to people and nations through the gifts of this church and every church. Give us your guidance to use all these gifts the best way we can. Amen.

Benediction
Flesh and blood cannot inherit the kingdom of God,
Only the imperishable can inherit the imperishable.
Let us go and live for the imperishable kingdom,
Sharing the news and our love with all others.
Amen.

Eighth Sunday after the Epiphany

Scripture
Isaiah 55:10-13
Psalm 92:1-4, 12-15
1 Corinthians 15:51-58
Luke 6:39-49

Call to Worship
One: It is good to give thanks to the LORD;
It is good to sing praises to your name, O Most High!
Many: We declare your steadfast love in the morning;
We proclaim your faithfulness by night.
One: We sing praises to the music of the lute and the harp;
We praise you to the melody of the lyre.
Many: Let our praises rise up to you,
May our praise tell of your holiness and mercy.
One: The righteous flourish like the palm tree;
They continually produce fruit.
Many: Their fruit shows that the LORD is upright.
God is the rock, there is no unrighteousness in God.

Invocation
LORD God, be our rock and our redeemer. Hear us as we sing to you, listen to the praises of our hearts. Help us to open ourselves to you during these moments that your Spirit may fill us and renew us. Amen.

Call to Confession
The blind cannot lead the blind. We have lived our lives following those who are spiritually blind, and we have been led into pits of sinfulness. Our very orientation and understanding of what is truly good is in question. We need to take time to confess.

Prayer of Confession
Our spiritual blindness has led us far from you, Great One. We have been so focused on the things this world has to offer that our minds have been far from the imperishable things that you offer us through Christ. Forgive us and renew us, we pray.

Assurance of Forgiveness
In Christ, death has lost its sting. In Christ, death has no victory. We sing the song of the redeemed when we are able to look boldly at ourselves

and ask God for forgiveness. In Christ there is forgiveness for all who repent. Thanks be to God.

Offertory Invitation
Jesus tells us that we will be judged by our fruit. What kinds of fruit are we creating in our lives? What kinds of fruit do we spend our time pruning and caring for? Through faithfulness to God's will, we begin to produce the fruit of God's blessing. Let us give that we may care for the things of God.

Offertory Prayer
Loving Creator, find us faithful in this offering we give to you. Help us to have wisdom, help us to have compassion, help us to have your eyes in the world that we may use these gifts where you desire us to use them. May all we do reflect your light to the world. Amen

Benediction
Be steadfast, be immovable, always excel in the work of the Lord.
When you work in the Lord, your work is never in vain.
May God's blessings be with you all this day and every day.
Amen.

Ninth Sunday after the Epiphany

Scripture
1 Kings 8:22-23, 41-43
Psalm 96:1-9
Galatians 1:1-12
Luke 7:1-10

Call to Worship
One: Ascribe to the LORD, all people,
Ascribe to the LORD both glory and strength.
Many: We give to the LORD the glory due to God's name.
We come into God's courts bringing our offerings.
One: Worship the LORD in holy splendor.
Worship the LORD and tremble before our God.
Many: The One God is great and greatly to be praised.
God is to be revered above all others.
One: Sing to the LORD your God,
Tell of the salvation God offers all your days.
Many: We declare God's glory among the nations.
We speak of God's marvelous work among all the peoples.

Invocation
God of all, may this worship space be set apart from the world. May it be a sanctuary where all else fades away except your love and your righteousness and our praise. In this time of worship help us to share in your glory, recognize your Spirit, and greatly grow our love for you.

Call to Confession
We have all in some ways traded the true gospel of Christ for a gospel of our own making. We have placed things or people or other idols above the LORD our God. In big and small ways we have sinned in this way against God. Let us pray for forgiveness.

Prayer of Confession
Lord, we are not worthy to have you come under our roofs. We have neglected your call and we have forgotten the call your gospel is on our lives. We come to you, asking for forgiveness, knowing that even though we are unworthy, you need only say the word and we will receive healing.

Assurance of Forgiveness
Forgiveness is offered to those who have the faithfulness to confess and

the faith to believe in the ability and will of Christ to give that forgiveness. In the act of forgiving and in the faith that Christ will forgive, we have received pardon for our sins. Praise God for this wonderful gift!

Offertory Invitation
In this time of offering, we are to give the very best we have to God. We do not come offering things of little value but offering the finest of what we possess and the best parts of who we are. May our offering be made in the spirit of true worship.

Offertory Prayer
Holy one, receive from us that which we have given to you this day. May what we have given here bless you in all the universe. Wherever we are found and wherever our gifts can reach, use all that we have and all that we are to offer your love to your creation. Amen.

Benediction
Grace to you and peace from our God in heaven and the Lord Jesus Christ,
Who gave himself for our sins to set us free from the present evil age, according to the will of God,
To whom be the glory forever and ever. Amen.

Ash Wednesday

Scripture
Joel 2:1-2, 12-17 or Isaiah 58:1-12
Psalm 51:1-17
2 Corinthians 5:20b-6:10
Matthew 6:1-6, 16-21

Call to Worship
One: We come this day to worship and to atone.
We come to offer ourselves back unto our God.
Many: Our many deeds stand ever before us,
Reminding us of the need for atonement and for healing.
One: God desires fasting, but not the fasting that causes strife.
God does not desire God's people to outwardly mortify themselves.
Many: Instead, God desires a fasting that releases the prisoners.
God desires that our fasting breaks the yoke of oppression.
One: When we share our bread with the poor and cover the naked, Our light shines forth like the dawn, and our healing is found in the LORD.
Many: May the LORD our God guide us continually and strengthen us.
May God use us to restore the streets and repair the breaches.

Invocation
LORD of all nations, fill this sanctuary with your presence, and fill us, your people, with the desire to do your justice throughout the world. Make our spirits one with yours that we would love your ways. Give us strength and ability to free this world from need and oppression. Amen.

Call to Confession
The LORD knows our sins, even those that we are unable or choose not to see. It is both a need and a privilege to confess our sins before God that we may receive healing. As a congregation and as individuals we offer our prayers to God.

Prayer of Confession
Have mercy on us, O God, according to your steadfast love. Wash us thoroughly from our iniquities and cleanse us from our guilt. We know our sins are ever before us. We know they are more numerous than even we recognize. You are justified in your sentence against us. But we cry out for mercy, trusting in your abundant grace. Save us, Holy One!

Assurance of Forgiveness
The sacrifice that is acceptable to God is a contrite heart and a broken spirit. When we allow ourselves to be broken in humble confession and when we bow before God, God is faithful to forgive. Through the atonement of Christ we have a gift we could never earn. Thanks to the Great Spirit over all!

Offertory Invitation
Our giving is not an act that is done in order to receive blessing for ourselves. Jesus commands that we not even allow our left hand to see what gifts our right hand is giving. We do not store up treasures on earth where they are destroyed, but rather in heaven where they are eternal. Let us give that others may be blessed and that the name of God may be lifted high!

Offertory Prayer
We have worshiped with our offering, and we pray that our offering is acceptable to you, O LORD. Take what we have, whether it has been given here or not, and use it and all we are to be a beacon of light in this world, a light that reflects your love for creation. Amen.

Benediction
Where your treasure is, there will your heart be also.
Let us store all our treasures in heaven, where they will be for us eternally.
In all things, let us proclaim the LORD our God!
Amen.

First Sunday of Lent

Scripture
Deuteronomy 26:1-11
Psalm 91:1-2, 9-16
Romans 10:8b-13
Luke 4:1-13

Call to Worship
One: You who live in the shelter of the Most High,
You who abide in the shadow of the Almighty, say to the LORD:
Many: You are my refuge, you are my strength.
The LORD is my God, in whom I trust.
One: Because the LORD is your refuge,
Because the Most High is your dwelling place,
Many: No evil shall befall God's people.
The LORD will protect those who put their trust in God.
One: For God has commanded the angels concerning God's people.
They will bear you up, so that you will not even dash your foot against a stone.
Many: The LORD delivers all those who love God.
The LORD satisfies them, and shows them God's salvation.

Invocation
All Faithful Giver of Life, you have given life to this world and to us, your people. You have called us to be your own. May your divine spirit be among us this day. May it nurture us, may it inspire us, may it lead us toward you and into greater service for you. Renew our hearts this day that they may be only yours. Amen.

Call to Confession
Temptation comes to all humans. It even came to Jesus the Christ. Jesus withstood temptation without sin, but we often cannot. We have allowed ourselves to be tempted, to be led astray, and we have sinned against one another and against the very master of the universe. Let us confess together.

Prayer of Confession
Our lives are filled with temptation, Great One, and we have followed after it. We recognize that we have been unfaithful to you and we have treated one another as objects to be used for our own gain. In many times we have taken the easy road instead of the blessed one. Please forgive us and help us to be better.

Assurance of Forgiveness
Scripture assures us that no one who believes in Jesus the Christ will be put to shame. Our belief leads us to love and repentance, and when we return to God with love and offer our repentance, we are healed from our sins. God is rich in grace!

Offertory Invitation
When the Israelites finally came into their promised land, a land that had great abundance for them, their first act was to give the very first of their fruits to the LORD as a sacrifice. Our land is abundant, but we often give of our leftovers. As we worship with our offering this day, let us give of the first and the best of all we have.

Offertory Prayer
May these, the fruits of our labors and the fruits of our talents, be used in a way that glorifies you, Loving God. We offer ourselves that your name may be glorified. Bless us and others near and far with the use of these gifts. Amen.

Benediction
There is no distinction between Jew and Greek, between human and human.
All are called into the saving grace we find in Christ Jesus.
May we shine that grace to all we see, all we meet, and all within our influence.
Amen.

Second Sunday of Lent

Scripture
Genesis 15:1-12; 17-18
Psalm 27
Philippians 3:17-4:1
Luke 13:31-35 *or Luke 9:28-36, (37-43a)*

Call to Worship
One: The LORD is our light and our salvation.
Of whom should we be afraid?
Many: The LORD is the stronghold of our lives.
There is no one whom we shall fear.
One: In the day of trouble, the LORD will hide us in God's shelter.
We seek to live in the house of the LORD all our days.
Many: Our hearts instruct us: "Seek the face of the LORD."
It is your face, Great One, that we seek.
One: Teach us your ways, O LORD, and lead us on a level path.
Show your goodness to your people.
Many: We wait for the LORD in strength.
Our hearts take courage in waiting for our God.

Invocation
There is none like you, Great and Holy Master of the Universe! Our very souls take delight in your presence here among us. Remind us of your commands, instruct us in your ways, and renew in us the sense of awe and wonder at your majesty. Rekindle in us the fires of service and devotion to you. Amen.

Call to Confession
We call ourselves God's people, but we have judged others and even judged one another within our own body of Christ. Jesus proclaimed and **Scripture** continually reminds us that we are not to judge others, yet we have imagined ourselves to have moral high ground and destroyed fellowship with God's children. We have much to confess.

Prayer of Confession
We appeal to your grace in this moment, Lord of All. Help us to focus in this time on ourselves, on our hearts, on our actions, and on our unfaithfulness. Keep us from the temptation of wondering how others may need to confess before you, and help us to confess our judgment, our malicious thoughts, and our lack of true forgiveness. Change these things in us, we pray.

Assurance of Forgiveness
Jesus taught that we cannot love God whom we cannot see if we cannot love one another. As we examine our hearts, let us turn to love and let us truly repent of our evil ways. If we can do this, God will be faithful to forgive and to heal. May this be God's will.

Offertory Invitation
The work of Christ had to be done, even in the midst of threats to his life. How much are we willing to give in order that our lives might shine the light of Christ? How much are we willing to risk for the sake of God's kingdom?

Offertory Prayer
May these gifts be offered to you humbly and without any regret. We pray that your goodness may fill our church and the world. May these gifts that we have given this day be used so that your love may overwhelm the land. Amen.

Benediction
Beloved, stand firm in the way of Christ,
Turning from the worldliness in which we are so often deeply embedded,
And instead choosing the way of love, shown to us in Christ Jesus.
May the Lord of all bless you and keep you. Amen.

Third Sunday of Lent

Scripture
Isaiah 55:1-9
Psalm 63:1-8
1 Corinthians 10:1-13
Luke 13:1-9

Call to Worship
One: O God, you are our God!
We seek you, indeed, our souls thirst for you!
Many: We long for you, as dry land longs for water.
We faint for the LORD of all.
One: We have beheld your power and glory,
As we have looked upon you in your sanctuary.
Many: Our lips praise you; your steadfast love is better than life.
We will bless you as long as we live.
One: We lift up our hands and call upon your name.
Our souls are satisfied as with a rich feast.
Many: For you have been our help, and our souls cling to you.
We sing for joy in the shadow of your wings.

Invocation
O Lord God, make your presence known to us and felt by us here in your sanctuary. Overwhelm us with your glory, and ignite within us a fire for you and for your desires for this world. Fill us with love for your people and the desire to serve them and to serve you with all we have. Amen.

Call to Confession
In many ways we have become idolaters, placing different things in the place that Christ is intended to occupy in our lives. We have sought after things that do not satisfy and neglected the will and the calling of Christ, the Lord of all the world. Let us confess our sinfulness.

Prayer of Confession
Hear our prayer to you, Gracious One! We have lost our way and have followed after things that cannot give us true happiness, nor can they give you glory. We have neglected the most important command you gave us, love of you and love of others, and we have instead chosen to place ourselves above all others and even above you. Forgive us and lead us in a new, better way.

Assurance of Forgiveness
Scripture tells us to seek the LORD while God may be found. Let the wicked forsake their ways, and the unrighteous forsake their thoughts. Let them return to the LORD, because the LORD desires to have mercy on us, and God will abundantly pardon all those who seek after righteousness.

Offertory Invitation
Why do we spend our money on things that are not good? Why do we throw our resources after things that do not satisfy? The desire of the LORD is that all may have food abundantly and things that are necessary for the abundance of life. We give that we may help to provide for those who do not have these things.

Offertory Prayer
Giving and loving God of all, may the gifts that we bring be used to feed your people, to show your love to the world, and to make your good news known beyond the reach of these doors. May we use the smallest amount to fulfill our needs so we can use the largest possible portion for the needs of others the world over. Amen.

Benediction
Go now into the world, bearing the fruit that God has called you to bear,
The fruit of love, the fruit of forgiveness, the fruit of generosity, and all other fruits
That the Spirit of God has given to you to share.
And may the God of all bless you as you bear your fruit for God's kingdom.
Amen.

Fourth Sunday of Lent

Scripture
Joshua 5:9-12
Psalm 32
2 Corinthians 5:16-21
Luke 15:1-3, 11b-32

Call to Worship
One: Happy are those whose transgressions are forgiven.
Happy are those whose sins are covered.
Many: When we keep our silence, our bodies waste away through groaning.
When we acknowledge our sin to God, God forgives our faults.
One: Let all who are faithful offer prayer to God.
At the time of distress, the waters will not reach them.
Many: God is a hiding place for us, preserving us from trouble.
The LORD surrounds us with glad cries of deliverance.
One: Instruct your people, faithful God. Teach us the way to go.
Counsel us, and always keep your eye upon us.
Many: We will be glad in the LORD and rejoice.
As we are righteous, we will shout for joy!

Invocation
LORD of all, you have made us new creations in you! Thank you for your work among us, your people! Reclaim us in this time of worship. Help us to set aside worldly needs and focus solely on your praise. Break open your Spirit in this sanctuary that when we leave this place we may be changed by our encounter with you. Amen.

Call to Confession
The psalmist reminds us how important it is to confess our sins before God. When we remain silent, our sin is ever with us, drying our strength. When we confess our iniquities, God hears our cries and God relieves us of our burdens. Let us confess our sins before our God.

Prayer of Confession
Our sins are ever before us, O God. We confess that we have not kept your covenant with us. We have misused your name, we have forgotten your commands, and we have hurt your people in active and passive ways. Forgive all we have done, and help us to learn of you that we may better follow your ways.

Assurance of Pardon
We learn in Scripture that the person who truly repents and who asks for forgiveness will receive it. God is faithful to this promise, and the promise is for any who are willing to set aside their ways of evil and move forward, doing their best to follow God's path. Let us be certain of our redemption this day.

Offertory Invitation
The gifts that God gives to the people are lavish ones. God spared nothing in reconciling us to God. Our gifts given back to God in gratitude and in service should be no less lavish. Only our best will do. We give now, and we hold nothing back from the Master of the universe.

Offertory Prayer
Nothing could be enough for our gifts to you, Awesome One. Even knowing this, we ask that you would receive these gifts, gifts of love, gifts of sacrifice, gifts of mercy, and that you would take them for the glory of your name wherever people are found. May we have wisdom and your blessing to use them for you. Amen.

Benediction
We have to celebrate! We, who were once lost, are now found!
We, who were once dead, have come to life!
Let us share the good news with all the world!
Amen.

Fifth Sunday of Lent

Scripture
Isaiah 43:16-21
Psalm 126
Philippians 3:4b-14
John 12:1-8

Call to Worship
One: When the LORD restored the fortunes of the Israelites,
They were like people who were dreaming.
Many: Their mouths were filled with laughter,
Their tongues were filled with shouts of joy.
One: Among all nations it was said,
"The LORD has done great things for them!"
Many: The LORD has done great things for us, God's people.
Let us rejoice and be glad in the LORD!
One: LORD God, fill our mouths with laughter!
Fill our tongues with shouts of joy for you.
Many: Let those who sow in tears reap in great joy!
LORD, continue to do great things for your people!

Invocation
Holy One, you proclaim through your prophet Isaiah that you are about to do new things. You will make ways for your people where there are none. You will make paths in the wilderness and in the rivers and in the desert. Make new pathways within our hearts, Great God, and draw us unto you as you meet us here in our time of worship. Amen.

Call to Confession
Whatever our qualifications, we do not have righteousness of our own. The only possibility we have for righteousness is the kind that we are given by Christ our Lord. That righteousness comes through faith, and in faith we turn to God in this time of confession.

Prayer of Confession
Creator of all, you have seen our ways. You know intimately our triumphs and our faults. You have seen where we have resisted temptation, and you have seen when we have not. Forgive our faults, all the sins we have committed in action or in speech or in any other way, and give us hearts of true repentance.

Assurance of Pardon
The grace of our Lord Jesus Christ abounds! It is greater by far than any sin we may have committed. When we turn to Christ for forgiveness and are truly sorry for things we have done against Christ and our neighbors, God is faithful to forgive, every single time. Thanks be to God!

Offertory Invitation
When Mary anointed Jesus with the costly perfume, she showed a devotion that was more important to her than any sum. Do we also have this devotion to Christ? Are we willing to give of ourselves and our possessions in the way Mary did? Let us faithfully worship God by giving of that which is costly to us.

Offertory Prayer
LORD, you have moved in us to give these gifts, now move in us to dedicate them solely to you. Help us to use all we have and all we are to share your love with all the people in this world. Let us be your hands and feet, let us act as Christ's body, sacrificing what we have to give ourselves to others. Amen.

Benediction
As we leave this place, let us press on toward the goal:
The goal of total devotion to Christ, forsaking other things we may consider gains, That the name of Christ may be known to all humankind. Amen.

Liturgy of the Palms

Scripture
Psalm 188:1-2, 19-29
Luke 19:28-40

Call to Worship
One: Give thanks to the LORD, for God is good!
God's steadfast love endures forever!
Many: Let the people say, "The LORD's steadfast love endures forever!"
May the LORD open the gates of righteousness to the people.
One: Let us enter God's gate of righteousness and give thanks to the LORD.
Thanks be to God for answering the people and becoming our salvation.
Many: The stone that the builders rejected has become the chief cornerstone.
This is the LORD's doing, and it is marvelous in our eyes.
One: This is the day that the LORD has made,
Let us rejoice and be glad in it!
Many: O give thanks to the LORD, for God is good!
God's steadfast love endures forever!

Invocation
As we invoke your Spirit in this sanctuary, Holy One, we recognize that it is we who are your guests in this place. Thank you for meeting us here and drawing us unto yourself. Release your Spirit into our hearts and minds, filling us with your love, and replacing our humanity with your perfect divinity. Amen.

Call to Confession
All people sin. This is a simple fact of the human condition. As God's people, we choose to work toward a better way, one that is as free from sin as possible. A starting point to a life of grace is the confessing of our sins and the willingness to truly repent. Let us confess those sins and resolve to repent before our God.

Prayer of Confession
God of all power, all wonder, and all grace, when we look upon our lives with eyes of truth, we see many ways that we have sinned against you and against your people. We have not loved you with our whole hearts, and we have not respected your ways, nor have we shown love to your people. Forgive us, we pray, and lead us forward in your righteous way.

Assurance of Forgiveness
God's grace and mercy extends to all those who call upon the name of the Lord. As a body and as individuals we have confessed our sins this day, and we have determined to keep from repeating them. In the name of Christ our Savior, we have been forgiven. Thanks be to God.

Offertory Invitation
When Jesus made his entry into Jerusalem, the people laid palm branches on the road and spread their own garments before him. As we enter into our time of offering, let us gratefully and generously lay our treasures at the feet of Jesus the Christ, who came that we might have salvation.

Offertory Prayer
Lord, our gifts are not worthy of you, but we pray that you would accept them. We ask for your blessing on these gifts and on this congregation. Help us to use our treasures and all we have to glorify you near and far.

Benediction
Let us go out shouting,
"Blessed is the King who comes in the name of the LORD!"
For if we do not proclaim Jesus, even the rocks will begin to cry out.
Let's go, proclaiming our Savior.
Amen.

Liturgy of the Passion

Scripture
Isaiah 50:4-9a
Psalm 31:9-16
Philippians 2:5-11
Luke 22:14-23:56 *or Luke 23:1-49*

Call to Worship
One: Christ is the Savior, the one who endured the passion for the sake of the people.
Christ is the example of perfect devotion to God.
Many: The LORD God opened Christ's ear, and Christ was not rebellious.
He did not turn away from the cup he was to drink.
One: Christ gave his back to those who struck him.
Christ gave his cheek to those who would pull out his beard.
Many: He did not hide his face from insults or from spitting,
Yet the LORD God was Christ's helper, and he did not suffer disgrace.
One: Christ set his face like flint, and was not put to shame.
God, the vindicator, was always near.
Many: It is the LORD God who was Christ's helper,
There were none who could declare him to be guilty.

Invocation
As we look upon this time of suffering, as we remember your great trials for the sake of humanity, LORD Christ, give us the gift of your Spirit. Help us to gain your morality, help us to know your pure devotion, and grant that we, too, may participate in your victory over death. Bless us in this time of worship that we might have a glimpse of you in your glory. Amen.

Call to Confession
The passion Christ suffered was for the sake of all humanity. All humans have sinned. It was humanity that crucified the ruler of the universe. Let us humbly approach God in confession for the sins we have committed, and let us sincerely pray for help to avoid sinfulness in our future.

Prayer of Confession
We are the builders who rejected the chief cornerstone. We are your people who rejected your Son. We are much the same as our ancestors who did not recognize the maker of the very world we live in, and sent him to his death. Forgive our lack of understanding. Forgive our

arrogance. Forgive our sinful disdain for you and for one another. Forgive us, we pray.

Assurance of Forgiveness
The God of all the cosmos is able to forgive, even when we have strayed so far as to condemn our own savior. People may be unfaithful, but God is never unfaithful. God has promised to forgive when we come to God in true repentance. Let us rejoice, that, sinful as we are, God has made us clean once again.

Offertory Invitation
How can we respond to a gift so wonderful as the gift of the Christ? How can we begin to give back to a God who has given so much for us? We must give of our very hearts, our very lives, our very selves. That is a gift that is acceptable to God.

Offertory Prayer
Our gifts are only a small portion of our true wealth, Great One, but we humbly offer them to you, praying that as you receive them they may bring healing to others. Help us to follow the example of Christ and be willing to give more—all we have—that your name may be glorified. Amen.

Benediction
As you leave this place,
Remember the blessing that you have received.
While we were still sinners, Christ was willing to suffer and die.
We have no claim to this gift, yet Christ gave freely anyway.
Go in awe and wonder at the awesome one we serve.

Resurrection of the Lord

Scripture
Acts 10:34-43 or Isaiah 65:17-25
Psalm 118:1-2, 14-24
1 Corinthians 15:19-26 or Acts 10:34-43
John 20:1-18 or Luke 24:1-12

Call to Worship
One: God says, "I am about to create new heavens and a new earth;
The former things shall not be remembered or come to mind.
Many: The people should be glad and rejoice forever in what I am creating.
I am about to create Jerusalem as a joy, and its people as a delight!
One: I will rejoice in Jerusalem.
No more shall the sound of weeping or the cry of distress be heard.
Many: The people shall never labor in vain or plant and another eat.
They will be offspring blessed by the LORD, with their descendants.
One: Before they call, I will answer;
While they are still speaking, I will hear them.
Many: There shall no longer be hurting or destruction on my holy mountain.
This is the word of the LORD.

Invocation
We rejoice before you this day, LORD of heaven and of earth. You have completed the work. You have won the victory. All you have done is glorious in our sight. We seek your presence here today that we may worship, that we may proclaim, that we may simply stand in awe of the wondrous and amazing thing you have done for us your people. Praise be to you alone, Great and Awesome God!

Call to Confession
It was for our sins that Jesus came to atone. The sins of the world were washed away as the victory was won by our Lord over death on that first Resurrection Sunday. With grateful hearts for the work of Christ and with sorrow over the sins we have committed, let us come to God with contrite hearts, confessing our sins.

Prayer of Confession
Glorious God and Savior of the world, we confess that while your promises to us have been kept perfectly, our conduct toward you and your

people has been anything but perfect. We have sinned against you in things we have done, things we have said, and things we have neglected. In the name of Jesus Christ our Savior, we ask for forgiveness and to be made whole once again.

Assurance of Forgiveness
It is in the name of Jesus the Christ that we are forgiven. It was the Christ who came to this world from glory. It was the Christ who taught the people how to live lives that glorified God. It was the Christ who suffered and died on the cross. And it was the Christ who won our victory through the resurrection. In the name of Christ, we are forgiven.

Offertory Invitation
How can we respond in any way other than sheer gratefulness for the wonderful gifts our God has given to us? How can we keep from generous giving and loving response as we remember the glorious resurrection? Let us worship God by giving of ourselves, that all God's children everywhere may know the wonder of our Savior.

Offertory Prayer
May these gifts that have been returned to you this day serve you in the way that you know to be best. Our vision is cloudy, our understanding dim, but you, O LORD, are perfect, and your ways are perfect. In your hands, may these gifts bring glory to you. Amen.

Benediction
The Good News of the gospel has been proclaimed here today.
Christ the Lord, who was dead, rose from the dead,
And through his rising, the world has been redeemed.
Let every knee bow and every tongue confess Jesus the Christ as Lord.
Amen.

Resurrection of the Lord (Alternative)

Scripture
Acts 10:34-43 or Isaiah 65:17-25
Psalm 118:1-2, 14-24
1 Corinthians 15:19-26 or Acts 10:34-43
John 20:1-18 or Luke 24:1-12

Call to Worship
One: Today we rejoice by singing glad songs of victory!
Christ the Lord is risen from the dead! Hallelujah!
Many: All the sins of the world have been overcome.
Christ has won the victory for us all!
One: We give thanks to the LORD for the steadfast love God has shown.
In God's mercy, we have been made free.
Many: Blessed be God, the Father, the Son, and the Holy Spirit,
Both now and forever more.
One: We live to proclaim the goodness of the LORD,
and the wonderful mystery of our salvation.
Many: Christ the Lord is risen!
He is risen indeed! Hallelujah!

Invocation
Come, risen Lord, be with us in this place of worship today. We stand in awe of your overwhelming love. We give all honor and glory and praise to you, the one who has redeemed the world through your victory over the grave. Fill our hearts this day with your love and mercy, and surprise us once more with your incredible grace. Amen.

Call to Confession
Christ is risen, and with his rising, the sins of the world have been taken away. Even though Christ has atoned for our sinfulness, we continue to sin in our lives. Let us confess our sins before the Triune God that God may know our hearts of repentance and God may forgive our sins.

Prayer of Confession
Infinite God, you see through all space and time. All moments to you are as one. We cannot begin to fully understand you. We do understand that you have called us to be your people, and in many ways, we have failed. We have not placed you first in our lives. We have envied and despised one another. In many other ways we have not been faithful to your call. Forgive us, we pray, and make us new once again.

Assurance of Forgiveness
The victory Christ has won this day is shared by all who believe in Jesus the Christ as their Lord and Savior. Jesus has promised when we ask for forgiveness and truly repent in our hearts, we will receive that forgiveness. Through Christ, we have been forgiven. Thanks be to God!

Offertory Invitation
Our blessings are too numerous to count. We have been given much, and we are assured that from those who are given much, much will be required. Let us come to this time of offering, recognizing our abundance with hearts willing to give for the sake of the healing of the world.

Offertory Prayer
Accept these gifts in your mercy, Gracious God. They are only a portion of what you have given us in blessing, but we pray for them, knowing that when you take them they can become something much greater than they are now. Use them, that the good news may spread across the globe. Amen.

Benediction
May the Lord of our ancestors,
the one who raised Jesus the Christ from the dead,
bless you this day as you strive to serve God and God's people.
May those blessings flow like life-sustaining waters to you,
and then through you to all you may encounter.
Amen.

Second Sunday of Easter

Scripture
Acts 5:27-32
Psalm 118:14-29 or Psalm 150
Revelation 1:4-8
John 20:19-31

Call to Worship
One: The LORD is our strength and our might.
The LORD has become our salvation.
Many: We sing the glad songs of victory,
"The right hand of the LORD is exalted!"
One: Blessed is the one who comes in the name of the LORD!
Our blessing comes from the house of the LORD.
Many: The LORD is our God, and the LORD has given us light.
That light is the light of all the world.
One: Sing praise to the one who comes in God's name.
Shout out glad praises to the LORD.
Many: You are our God, and we give our thanks to you.
We give thanks to the LORD for God is good, God's steadfast love endures forever!

Invocation
Help us to focus our hearts and minds on you in this time of worship, wonderful God. You have brought us here to experience your presence, and we call upon you to meet with us here. We ask for your Spirit to be present in all we say and do, that we may be changed by encountering you in this sanctuary. Amen.

Call to Confession
As we prepare to confess our sins before God, we remember that it is in the confessing of our sins that we can be forgiven. In thankfulness for that promise, and in sincere repentance before God, let us confess as a body the ways we have been unfaithful to God's call on our lives.

Prayer of Confession
Lord of all, hear our prayer, and have mercy. We have sinned against you. We have placed other things first in our lives. We have forgotten to honor you with all our hearts. We have neglected to love you with all our souls, minds, and strength. Forgive us, we pray, and help our repentance to be real and permanent.

Assurance of Forgiveness
Jesus Christ is the faithful witness, the firstborn of the dead, and Christ has freed us from our sins through his atonement. Because of the love of Christ, we have the ability to go to God, confessing our sins, in confidence that those sins are forgiven by a loving and gracious Christ. Thanks be to God!

Offertory Invitation
Jesus said that those who have not seen him and have yet believed in him are greatly blessed. We have not seen the risen savior in the way Thomas and the other apostles did, but as we worship now by giving of our time, talents, and treasure, we proclaim our faith in the love of Christ our savior. Let us give generously.

Offertory Prayer
We dedicate our gifts and ourselves to you, Holy One. May the things we have given in this time and may all we have and all we are be dedicated to you, that your love may spread to all people and that the wonder of the resurrection may be known everywhere. Amen.

Benediction
Peace be with you. As the father sent Jesus, and as Jesus sent the Apostles,
So we, too, are sent to proclaim the love of God in Jesus the Christ.
Go now, and receive blessings through Christ our Lord.
Amen.

Third Sunday of Easter

Scripture
Acts 9:1-6 (7-20)
Psalm 30
Revelation 5:11-14
John 21: 1-19

Call to Worship
One: We extol you, O LORD. You have lifted us up.
We cried to you for help, and you have healed us.
Many: Sing praises to the LORD, O you faithful ones!
Give great thanks to God's holy name.
One: Praise the LORD, for God's favor lasts a lifetime.
Weeping may last for the night, but joy comes in the morning!
Many: By your favor, O LORD, you have established your people.
You have made us like a strong mountain.
One: O LORD, you have turned our mourning into dancing!
You have clothed us with great joy!
Many: May our souls praise you and never be silent.
O LORD, our God, we will give you thanks forever!

Invocation
Worthy are you, O God. You are great and mighty in power. You have shown us your wonders and your signs. You have shown us the great worth in your son Jesus the Christ. You have sent us the advocate to care for and guide us. Renew us this day and make us once again yours and only yours. Amen.

Call to Confession
Paul considered himself unworthy to be called an apostle because he had persecuted the church, yet through God's grace, he became a mighty apostle. Peter denied the Lord Jesus three times during his trials. The greatest among us are still sinners. Let us confess that we, too, may be made whole through grace.

Prayer of Confession
God of all times and places, we call ourselves your people, but we have often not acted as if this were true. Our conduct toward each other is filled with jealousy and anger and bitterness. Our love toward you seems strong one moment and practically absent the next. Please forgive us, and in your mercy heal us again.

Assurance of Forgiveness
When we repent before God, God is faithful to forgive. When we confess that we love God, God claims our love and reminds us that our message of hope is one that is to be shared with all God's sheep. We are forgiven, and we are called again to serve.

Offertory Invitation
The calling to the life of a disciple is not guaranteed to be an easy one. Often God calls servants to a life that is filled with suffering for the sake of the Christ. Faithful service sometimes requires great sacrifice. Let us be faithful to that calling.

Offertory Prayer
Lord Jesus, you know our hearts, you know our possessions, you know our talents. Grant that we may use all these things with which you have blessed us that your name may be known in our world, that your will may be done in this world, and that your kingdom of peace may be found on earth as it is in heaven. Bless our giving, that it may bless your sheep.

Benediction
To the one seated on the throne,
And to the Lamb
be blessing and honor and glory and might forever and ever.
May the very same God bless you as you strive to serve.
Amen.

Fourth Sunday of Easter

Scripture
Acts 9:36-43
Psalm 23
Revelation 7:9-17
John 10:22-30

Call to Worship
One: The LORD is our shepherd.
We shall not want.
Many: The LORD makes us lie down in green pastures.
The LORD leads us beside still waters.
One: God restores our souls.
God leads us in right paths for the sake of God's name.
Many: Even though we may walk through the darkest valley, we fear no evil,
For you are with us; your rod and your staff, they comfort us.
One: You prepare a table before us in the presence of our enemies.
You anoint our heads with oil; our cups overflow.
Many: Surely goodness and mercy shall follow us all the days of our lives,
And we shall live in the house of the LORD our whole lives long.

Invocation
The glorious song of the redeemed is sung at your throne, Great God! "Blessing and glory and wisdom and thanksgiving and honor and power and might be to our God forever and ever!" Enter into this place with all your glory and renew in us spirits to serve you, the one all-powerful God of the cosmos! Amen.

Call to Confession
We have been told about God and about the Christ and about the Spirit, but have we truly believed? We know what God considers to be good conduct and upright living, but have we worked to live in this way? As hard as we may have tried, we are still guilty of sin. Let us confess before our God.

Prayer of Confession
Lord of the heavens and of the earth, we confess that we have sinned against you and against your people. In our thoughts, in our words, and in our actions, we have missed the mark set for us by you and by your son, Jesus. Please forgive us and help us to be more like our savior.

Assurance of Forgiveness
The great multitude in heaven sings, "Salvation belongs to our God who is seated on the throne and to the Lamb!" Salvation is God's, and God has promised to give salvation to those who humbly repent and ask to be forgiven of their sins. For all you have confessed this day, you have been made free.

Offertory Invitation
We give, not out of obligation, but as a sign of the love we have for Jesus the Christ. We give, not expecting blessings in return, but in hopeful expectation of blessings for our neighbors here and around the world. We give, expressing great faithfulness and love for our Lord and Savior.

Offertory Prayer
We have worshiped you in song, in prayer, in silence, and now in the giving of our gifts this day. May these gifts be acceptable to you, and may they be a blessing to all others throughout the world in whatever way is most pleasing to you, Great One. Amen.

Benediction
May the Lamb be your shepherd,
Calling you as part of his flock,
and may Christ's blessings be with you
from this day forward, forevermore.
Amen.

Fifth Sunday of Easter

Scripture
Acts 11:1-18
Psalm 148
Revelation 21:1-6
John 13:31-35

Call to Worship
One: Praise the LORD! Praise the LORD from the heavens;
Praise God in the heights, all angels, Praise God all hosts!
Many: Praise the LORD, sun and moon, Praise God all you shining stars!
Praise the LORD, you highest heavens, and you waters above the heavens!
One: Let them praise the name of the LORD,
for God commanded and they were created.
Many: God established them forever and ever.
The LORD fixed their boundaries which cannot be passed.
One: Praise the LORD, sea monsters, all deeps, fire and hail, snow and frost,
Stormy winds, Mountains and hills, fruit trees and cedars, all creeping animals and birds.
Many: Kings of all the earth, all people, young and old, praise the name of the LORD.
God's name alone shall be exalted; the glory of the LORD is above heaven and earth.

Invocation
Almighty and everlasting God, you have promised us that one day all things will be made complete. In that day, humans will fully dwell in the presence of God. As we come to this sanctuary to worship you, we ask that you may dwell among us as completely as possible in this age. Fill our spirits, pour into this space, and cause us to recognize your Spirit in and among us. Amen.

Call to Confession
Jesus called us to love one another in the same way that Jesus loved us. That is a command that is all but impossible for humans to live out every moment of every day. In our humanity we all fail to love in the way Jesus commanded. We all need to be forgiven for these failings. Let us confess before our God.

Prayer of Confession
Lord of all people, you have called us into love for you and love for all others. We have the best intentions to fulfill this call, but we have been unable to do so completely. We have misplaced our loyalty to you at times, and we have neglected others' needs. When we have done this, we have sinned against you and against your commands for us. In your grace, please forgive, that we may be healed.

Assurance of Forgiveness
The grace of the Lord Jesus Christ is sufficient for all of us. No matter where we have been, no matter what we have done, no matter how we have sinned, God has made a pathway to wholeness for all of us. When we repent of our sins, Christ intercedes on our behalf. In the name of Christ, you are forgiven!

Offertory Invitation
Christ's love for the world was a sacrificial one. He was willing to give of the great riches that he had in glory so that the people of the world may receive healing and salvation. We are called by Jesus to love as he loved. In that spirit of love, let us give that others may receive the word of Christ and their daily needs.

Offertory Prayer
We lay our sacrifices before you, Great and Mighty God. We ask you for your blessings. Bless us with wisdom to know how to use these gifts. Bless the gifts themselves that they may reach far into your world. Bless us with generous hearts that we may ever continue to give. Amen.

Benediction
Jesus commanded those who followed him to love one another as he loved them.
Let us go forward into the world, sharing the love of Christ with all we know and meet.
Amen.

Sixth Sunday of Easter

Scripture
Acts 16:9-15
Psalm 97
Revelation 21:10, 22-22:5
John 14:23-29 *or John 5:1-9*

Call to Worship
One: May God be gracious to us and bless us.
May the LORD's face shine upon us.
Many: That God's way may be known upon the earth,
And that God's saving power would be known among all nations.
One: Let the peoples praise you, O God, let all peoples praise you!
Let all nations be glad and sing for joy.
Many: Let them be glad, for you judge the nations with equity,
and you guide all the nations upon the earth.
One: The earth has yielded its increase;
God, our God, has blessed us!
Many: May God continue to bless us,
let all the ends of the earth revere the LORD!

Invocation
We bow before you, awesome and mighty God, in thanksgiving for your blessings to us and in hope and expectation of your guidance. Meet us here in your sanctuary this day. Fill us with your Spirit that we may know you better and understand your desires from us more fully. Renew our dedication to you in this time of worship. Amen.

Call to Confession
Through the ages, the messages of God's servants have convicted those within the community and those who were outside the church of their failure to properly serve God. When they have been convicted, they have confessed and repented of their sins. Today we are called to that same time of confession.

Prayer of Confession
Holy and Loving God, we are saddened to acknowledge our sins before you. When we look on our lives we see how we have neglected your calls to us. Our way has not been straight, our pathways have been winding. Forgive us now and grant that we may do our best to serve you rightly in our future.

Assurance of Forgiveness
The Holy Spirit intercedes for us. Although all sin and fall short of the way God has set before us, the advocate strengthens us, and Jesus the Christ offers forgiveness and salvation to those who repent. When we confess our sins and determine to realign ourselves with God's way, we are forgiven.

Offertory Invitation
The riches of Christ's glory were given freely to us in his life, death, and resurrection. We can do nothing to repay Jesus the Christ for his love, and we would be foolish to try. Instead, we make offerings in love that the word of Christ may reach to the ends of the earth.

Offertory Prayer
Lord, receive these offerings. Make them blessings to you. Make them blessings to all your people. May all we have and all we are, whether it is offered here or not, be used for the uplifting of your name throughout the globe. Amen.

Benediction
As Jesus gave these blessings to his disciples, so they are for us,
Peace I leave with you, my peace I give to you.
I do not give as the world gives to you.
Do not let your hearts be troubled, and do not let them be afraid.
Amen.

Seventh Sunday of Easter

Scripture
Acts 16:16-34
Psalm 97
Revelation 22:12-14, 16-17, 20-21
John 17:20-26

Call to Worship
One: The LORD is king! Let the earth rejoice!
Let all the nations of the world be glad!
Many: Clouds and thick darkness are all around our God.
Righteousness and justice are the foundation of God's throne.
One: The mountains melt like wax before the LORD of all the earth.
The heavens proclaim God's righteousness, and all people behold God's glory.
Many: The peoples of the world hear and are glad.
All nations rejoice in your judgments, O God.
One: For you, O God, are most high above all the earth.
You are exalted far above any other.
Many: Light dawns for the righteous and joy for the upright in heart.
Rejoice in the LORD, O you righteous, and give thanks to God's holy name!

Invocation
You alone are holy, LORD of all the universe. You alone are to be worshiped and adored. You alone are the most high, who reigns along with your Son and the Holy Spirit. Make this sanctuary a place where your Spirit enters into the world and enters into our hearts. Move in us this day that we would know you as our LORD and God. Amen.

Call to Confession
The sinfulness of humanity is ever before us. God knows all our deeds, those of which we can be proud, and those that we are ashamed to admit. In this time of confession, we come before God to free ourselves of the burdens of our misdeeds and to God for forgiveness through Christ. Let us pray together.

Prayer of Confession
Gracious One, we recognize our sinful ways. We have made choices that are not in keeping with your will for our lives. In countless ways we have forgotten the things that you have commanded are most important and

sought after things that do not satisfy. In your faithfulness, forgive your servants, and give us strength and wisdom to be better disciples.

Assurance of Forgiveness
Christ invites all those who are thirsty to come. Christ invites all who wish to take of the water of life to drink freely. When we turn our eyes on Jesus and repent of the things we have done that are outside God's path for us, we have drawn from the water, and it has cleansed and redeemed us. Thanks be to God.

Offertory Invitation
What shall we do in return for all Christ has done for us? What shall we give in loving response to the gift of living water? We are called to give all we can of our efforts, of our treasures, and of our very selves that Christ may be glorified. Let us give, keeping the gifts of Christ ever in our minds and hearts.

Offertory Prayer
Great Savior of all, we return to you this day a portion of the blessings that you have given to us. We are grateful for your gifts, and we pray that these gifts may be a blessing back to you. Give us wisdom to use them to your glory and give us hearts for giving in all our days. Amen.

Benediction
Jesus prayed that the fellowship would be one.
Let us go into the world, united with all our sisters and brothers in Christ,
Offering love and honor to a world in need,
as one body, the body of Christ.
Amen.

Ascension of the Lord

Scripture
Acts 1:1-11
Psalm 47 *or Psalm 93*
Ephesians 1:15-23
Luke 24:44-53

Call to Worship
One: Clap your hands, all you peoples;
Shout to God with loud songs of joy!
Many: For the LORD, the most high, is awesome.
God is the great king over all the earth.
One: Sing praises to God, sing praises!
God has gone up with a shout, the LORD with the sound of a trumpet!
Many: Sing praises to our ruler, the one and only God!
For God is the king over all the earth.
One: God is king over all nations;
God sits on the holiest of thrones.
Many: Sing, clap, shout to the LORD our God,
For God is great and is greatly to be praised!

Invocation
LORD of all, you are great indeed. Your glory reaches into all places in the universe. Let your glory and wonder reach into this worship space, changing this place from an earthly space to a holy and heavenly one. Transform our world, transform our sanctuary and transform our hearts by your wonderful presence here. Amen.

Call to Confession
We who love the Lord are called to remember the ways that we have sinned. God has promised to forgive our sins when we openly and honestly confess them and humble ourselves before God in repentance. Let us offer our words of confession together.

Prayer of Confession
God, you are holy. There is no shadow of iniquity in you. You know our thoughts, our deeds, and all our ways. We confess that we have been unable to live perfectly according to your standards. We have sinned by not loving our sisters and brothers. We have sinned by placing idols in our lives in the place you should hold alone. Forgive us, and give us the strength to truly repent.

Assurance of Forgiveness
As Jesus was about to ascend to the heavens, he reminded the disciples that the Christ was sent into the world for the forgiveness of sins. Those who turn to God, confessing their sins and choosing to repent have already been forgiven in the name of Jesus the Christ. Thanks be to God!

Offertory Invitation
God is ruler over all things, all principalities, all nations, and all people. All we have ultimately belongs to God. God has called us to use those gifts given by God to be the body of Christ in the world. Let us give that we may heal, comfort, and care for all in need.

Offertory Prayer
We give thanks, gracious God, for the gifts you have given to us, and we ask for your blessing on these gifts we have returned to you. Please help your servants to use all we have and all we can be as blessings to your people wherever they are. Amen.

Benediction
Let us go, with our eyes enlightened,
that we may proclaim the risen Savior in every way we can,
in every place we can, with all the means we can.
Go with the blessings of a wonderful God.
Amen.

Day of Pentecost

Scripture
Acts 2:1-21 *or Genesis 11:1-9*
Psalm 104 24-34, 35b
Romans 8:14-17 *or Acts 2:1-21*
John 14:8-17, (25-27)

Call to Worship
One: O LORD, how manifold are your works!
In wisdom you have made them all, the earth is full of your creatures!
Many: Your creation fills the seas, O God,
The land and the air are full of the works of your hands.
One: All these look to you for their food in due season.
When you give to them from your hand, they gather it up.
Many: When you send forth your spirit, the world is renewed.
From you, O God, is the world filled with good things.
One: May the glory of the LORD endure forever;
May our meditations be pleasing to our God.
Many: We will sing to the LORD as long as we live.
Bless the LORD; let us sing praise to our God as long as we have breath!

Invocation
Your love, O LORD, reaches farther than human minds can begin to understand. Your glory is made known throughout all creation. Your Spirit is present in all times and in all places, filling the world with the gift of life. We call upon your Spirit this day, this moment, to renew us, to fill us with life again, to bless us with a re-making of our hearts and minds in your image. Amen.

Call to Confession
In the time of Babel, the people sinned by trying to be as high as God. In many ways the source of our continuing sinfulness is trying to be greater than humans can be. In our conceit we forget how much we need God and need one another. Let us pray for forgiveness.

Prayer of Confession
God of all times and places, we confess that we have sinned against you and against your creation. Our sin is before us even now, reminding us of the ways that we have fallen short of your calling on our lives. Help us to reconcile with you and with all others, and help us to be more like our Savior, Jesus.

Assurance of Forgiveness
We have not received a Spirit of slavery to sin, but one of forgiveness of sins and freedom from sin. When we are able to rely on God and truly repent of the ways we have sinned, we will always be forgiven. Thanks be to God for that wonderful assurance!

Offertory Invitation
The gift of God's Spirit moved the disciples to do wondrous, amazing things. We pray that the gift of God's Spirit into our lives and into this place will inspire us to do wonderful things for God's kingdom on earth. Let us give, with the faith given by God's Holy Spirit.

Offertory Prayer
Holy God, we lay our gifts before you. You have given these things to us, and as we return them to you, we pray that they may not only be acceptable to you, but that they may truly make a difference in the lives of people throughout the globe. Help us to use these gifts and all our gifts in ways that honor you. Amen.

Benediction
Jesus told his disciples that the one who believes in him will also do the works that Jesus does.
In fact, Jesus says, they will do even greater works than Jesus could then do, because he was going to ascend to heaven. Let us go, believing in Christ, and doing Christ's work in the world. Amen.

Trinity Sunday (First Sunday after Pentecost)

Scripture
Proverbs 8:1-4; 22-31
Psalm 8
Romans 5:1-5
John 16:12-15

Call to Worship
One: O LORD, our Sovereign, how majestic is your name in all the earth!
You have set your glory above the heavens.
Many: When I look at your heavens, the work of your fingers,
The moon and the stars you have established;
One: What are human beings that you are mindful of them?
Who are mortals, that you care for them?
Many: Yet you have made people a little lower than God.
You have crowned humanity with honor and glory.
One: You have given humans dominion over the works of your hands.
You have placed all things under their feet.
Many: Sheep and oxen, beasts, birds of the air, creatures of the sea.
O LORD, our Sovereign, how majestic is your name in all the earth.

Invocation
We have come to hear your voice of wisdom, great One. We are here in worship to be filled with the awe and wonder of your presence. Creator God renew us with affection for all your creation. Savior God give us faith and gratitude for your gift of redemption. Spirit God, work within us and through us that we may be vessels of your gifts to the rest of our world. Great Three-In-One, we worship you. Amen.

Call to Confession
Wisdom has been sent to us and among us, crying out, and teaching us the paths of righteousness. Even though our hearts are often willing to be what God has called us to be, we still make mistakes and veer from God's way. Let us confess our sins before our God.

Prayer of Confession
Wonderful, Almighty, and gracious God, we confess that we have not been the holy and righteous people you have called us to be. We have broken your commands. We have forsaken your laws. We have hurt one another and ignored you. Bring us once again into your fold, and help us to set aside our sinful ways, that we may follow you with all we are.

Assurance of Forgiveness
Paul writes that we have been justified by faith, and because of this, we have peace with God through our Lord Jesus the Christ. When we acknowledge our sin and truly repent, we are forgiven through the faith we have in the healing power of Christ. We can be confident in this promise this day and every day.

Offertory Invitation
We have received many gifts from the source of all things, the God of the entire universe. In this time of worship, we have the opportunity to return to God some of the gifts that we have been given in faithful worship and in thoughtful generosity. Let us make the most of this opportunity.

Offertory Prayer
Giver of all, we remember your gifts to us even as we take time to give our gifts back to you. Receive these gifts, Holy God. Bless them with your Spirit. Make them vessels of your healing and bearers of your grace to the entire world, wherever our influence can reach. Amen.

Benediction
Go now,
Celebrating the Trinity:
The Creator, the Savior, and the Holy Spirit,
And may the great Three in One bless you as you strive to live a life of service to God and to humanity.
Amen.

Proper 3

Scripture
Isaiah 55:10-13
Psalm 92:1-4, 12-15
1 Corinthians 15:51-58
Luke 6:39-49

Call to Worship
One: It is good to give thanks to the LORD,
To sing praises to your name, O Most High!
Many: It is good to declare your steadfast love in the morning,
And your faithfulness by night.
One: It is our privilege to sing to you to the music of the lute,
To the sounds of the harp and the melody of the lyre.
Many: For you, O LORD, have made your people glad by your work.
At the works of your hands I sing for joy!
One: The righteous flourish like the palm tree,
In their old age, they still produce their fruits.
Many: Their fruits show that the LORD is upright.
God is our rock, there is no unrighteousness in our God.

Invocation
God of heaven, you are our rock and our fortress. In you there is no corruption, only perfection. Visit this place in this time of worship. Renew our commitments to you. Rekindle the fire for your work and your will. Cause us to set aside other concerns and be simply yours. Amen.

Call to Confession
Jesus asked why people would look at the speck in the eye of another while ignoring the log in their own eye. When we live without confession, we are like those who ignore something in their own eye. Let us do our best to remove the sin from ourselves and refrain from our judgment of others.

Prayer of Confession
LORD of all, God of the universe, and keeper of our souls, we turn to you now in prayer for forgiveness of the sins we have committed. We have wandered from you. We have judged others for their sin while ignoring our own. Forgive us, we pray, and give us hearts for true repentance.

Assurance of Forgiveness
Death has been swallowed up by the love of Jesus the Christ. Although the sting of death is sin, and the power of sin is the law, in Christ we have been made new creations, freed from the law. When we confess our sins before God, through God's grace we are redeemed. Rejoice in the LORD!

Offertory Invitation
Those who build on a solid foundation will be well served when the tempests of life arise. Floods cannot shake them, winds cannot damage. We give now in testimony that the foundation of our lives is found in God and in no other being or idol.

Offertory Prayer
We set aside these gifts specifically for your purposes in the world. LORD, bless these gifts and cause them to be used to your glory. Bless all of us now, that we may dedicate not only these gifts, but all we have in order that the good news may be known across the globe. Amen.

Benediction
Go today, beloved, being steadfast, immovable, and always excelling in the work of the Lord, because you know that in the Lord your labor is not in vain.
Amen.

Proper 4

Scripture
1 Kings 18:20-21, (22-29), 30-39
Psalm 96
or
1 Kings 8:22-23, 41-43
Psalm 96:1-9
Galatians 1:1-12
Luke 7:1-10

Call to Worship
One: Sing to the LORD a new song!
Sing to the LORD, all the earth.
Many: We sing to the LORD and we bless God's holy name.
We will tell of God's salvation from day to day.
One: Declare God's glory among all nations.
Declare God's marvelous works before all people.
Many: For great is the LORD, and greatly to be praised!
All the gods of the peoples are idols, but the LORD made the heavens!
One: Honor and majesty are before our God.
Strength and beauty are in the sanctuary of the LORD most high.
Many: Ascribe to the LORD the glory due God's name and bring an offering into God's courts.
Worship the LORD in holy splendor; tremble before God, all the earth.

Invocation
Throughout the ages, Great God of all the universe, you have proven yourself to be the one true God, the only one with power and majesty and wisdom. Turn our hearts to you this day. Turn our minds to your praise alone. Enter this sanctuary with great might that when we leave this place, we will have been changed by an encounter with the God of the entire cosmos. Amen.

Call to Confession
As individuals and as communities we have often followed a different God from the one that we have come here to worship. Our adoration for things may not be as egregious as the people's worship of the false god Ba'al, but any time we place other things higher in our priority than worship of God, we have sinned. Let us confess before God.

Prayer of Confession
Holy God of all, we confess that we have often worshiped the idols of wealth, the idols of success, and many other idols that we have placed before you in our lives. We truly repent of these ways, and we ask for your help to set aside anything that comes between us and our worship of you. Help us to set the things of this world aside that you alone may be worshiped wherever we are.

Assurance of Forgiveness
We know that we are not worthy for the Lord to visit with us and to heal us, yet in faith, we know that Christ need only say the word, and we shall be healed. Jesus' life, death and resurrection proclaims that it is Christ's will that we be healed. When we ask in faith, we are forgiven. Thanks be to God!

Offertory Invitation
All who recognize the LORD as the ruler of their lives are called to participate in the gifts of the church. We give so that others may be healed. We give so that we may be found faithful. We give that the glory of God, the grace of Christ, and the power of the Holy Spirit may be known throughout the universe. Let us give faithfully.

Offertory Prayer
Before you, O LORD, we lay our gifts. We pray that you would accept them as faithful and humble offerings to you. Please use all we have given and inspire us to give more of our treasures and ourselves that your name and your kingdom would be lifted in all the earth. Amen.

Benediction
Receive the blessings of God the creator,
God the Christ and Savior,
and God the Holy Spirit.
May the word of God inspire you, your faith in God sustain you, and your love of God stir you to action in the name of Christ Jesus.
Amen.

Proper 5

Scripture
1 Kings 17:8-16, (17-24) *or 1 Kings 17:17-24*
Psalm 146 *or Psalm 30*
Galatians 1:11-24
Luke 7:11-17

Call to Worship
One: Praise the LORD! Praise the LORD, O my soul!
Do not place your trust in mortals, in whom there is no help.
Many: We will praise the LORD as long as we live!
We will sing praises to our God our whole lives long.
One: Happy are those whose help is the God of Jacob.
Happy are all whose hope is in the LORD their God.
Many: For God made the heavens and the earth
God made the seas and all that is in them.
One: God executes justice, feeds the hungry, frees the prisoners.
God opens the eyes of the blind and lifts up those who are bowed down.
Many: The LORD loves the righteous and watches over strangers,
upholding widows and orphans.
The LORD will reign forever, our God, for all generations. Praise the LORD!

Invocation
You are awesome, mighty and wonderful God. You will reign forever, caring for your people, lifting up the downtrodden, and rescuing those in distress. We come today to meet with you. We come to worship you. We come to know you better, that you might better guide us, your people. We worship you in wholeness and in truth. Amen.

Call to Confession
The gospel of Christ is that those who are not perfectly righteous, all humanity, in fact, have their hope for salvation through the love and grace found in Christ Jesus. Our time of confession is our opportunity to confess to God for our sins as people and as communities, that God may forgive and we may be redeemed. Let us pray together.

Prayer of Confession
Great and loving God, we confess that we are imperfect people. We have been unable to keep your commands perfectly, and when we have stumbled, by accident or by choice, we have sinned against you. We come

before you now, humbly asking for forgiveness of those sins, and praying that you may help us to follow you more closely in our future.

Assurance of Forgiveness
Our Lord, the Lord Jesus the Christ, is a savior of great compassion. Jesus has promised that when we truly repent of our sins, confessing them to God through Jesus, we will be forgiven, and we will receive redemption. This is the good news of Christ's gospel. Thanks be to God!

Offertory Invitation
The gifts of God are too numerous to count. God's blessings flood our world every day, and we have been fortunate enough to experience many of those gifts in our own lives. Let us turn now, with hearts filled with gratitude, to give back to God for God's work in our world.

Offertory Prayer
In your mercy, God of all, receive these gifts given to you out of the bounty you have given to us. Give us hearts to use all our gifts to care for your people, and help us to use not only our treasures, but our very selves for your glory. Amen.

Benediction
Jesus preached a message of comfort for those who were afraid or sad.
To all who mourn, Jesus says, "Do not weep!"
Instead, Christ invites us to live in excitement and happiness for the kingdom coming into our world.
Go, living this blessing in all your lives!
Amen.

Proper 6

Scripture
1 Kings 21:1-10, (11-14) 15-21a or 2 Samuel 11:26-12:10, 13-15
Psalm 5:1-8 or Psalm 32
Galatians 2:15-21
Luke 7:36-8:3

Call to Worship
One: Give ear to our words, O LORD.
Give heed to our sighing and our calling out to you.
Many: Listen to the sounds of our cries, Great God.
For we pray to you alone, our King and our God.
One: In the morning, O LORD, you hear our voice.
In the morning, we speak to you, and we listen to hear your voice.
Many: You are not a God who delights in wickedness,
Instead, you are a God who loves righteousness.
One: Help us to walk in righteousness,
That, through the abundance of your steadfast love, we may enter your house.
Many: We bow down before you in awe of your majesty.
Lead us, LORD, and make your way straight before us.

Invocation
God of Creation, you have made us all and you have called us to be your servants. We have come to worship you, and we pray that your Spirit would be in this house, moving within and among us, and causing us to be energized for the work you have given. Change our hearts, O God. Replace them with your own heart for love, for service, and for one another. Amen.

Call to Confession
It is not through the law that we will be justified, but through grace alone. The grace offered to us by Jesus Christ is reliant on our honest confession of our sins and our true repentance. We take this time in worship to truly recognize our sins and to ask for forgiveness. Let us confess together.

Prayer of Confession
God of all, we confess that we have not followed the way you have placed before us. We have been so focused on our own wants and desires and our own comfort that we have neglected those around us who are in need. We have forgotten to give you our first fruits and place you first in our lives. Forgive us, we pray, and lead us forward in righteousness.

Assurance of Forgiveness
Our justification comes not through adherence to the law or any good deeds, but through the love and grace of Jesus the Christ. When we confess our sins and truly repent, we are forgiven through the love that Christ gave to the world. Let us rejoice in this wonderful assurance of our pardon!

Offertory Invitation
Our gifts to God are intended to be thoughtful and sacrificial. When we approach God's throne to give what we have to the Lord Christ, we should be certain that we are giving all we can to remake the world in the way God desires. Let us give, gratefully embracing the possibilities for change that our gifts can bring.

Offertory Prayer
We offer our gifts to you, wonderful God, and we pray that they may be acceptable to you. Use them in whatever way is pleasing to you. May they heal the sick, restore sight to the blind, renew the spirit of the lost, and bring this world closer to becoming the kingdom you have begun in Christ Jesus.

Benediction
Jesus says to those who love and honor God,
"Your faith has saved you; go in peace."
Let us go into the world, rejoicing in this promise, and sharing the wonders of God's world with all others.
Amen.

Proper 7

Scripture
1 Kings 19:1-4, (5-7), 8-15a *or Isaiah 65:1-9*
Psalm 42 and Psalm 43 *or Psalm 22:19-28*
Galatians 3:23-29
Luke 8:26-39

Call to Worship
One: As a deer longs for flowing streams,
So our souls long for you, O God!
Many: Our souls thirst for God, the one true and living God.
When shall we come and behold God's face?
One: Why are you cast down, O my soul?
Hope in God, for we shall praise the LORD alone.
Many: O LORD, send out your light and truth; let them lead us.
Let them bring us to your holy hill and to your dwelling.
One: Then we shall go to the altar of God, to God, our exceeding joy!
Let us go to praise God with the harp and with songs of worship.
Many: Our souls thirst for you, O God!
May we meet with you and be quenched!

Invocation
We welcome you into this space, holy and everlasting God! We have come to worship you alone. We lift up our voices and wonder at the awesome and loving God that you are. Help us to recognize you in this time of worship, whether in an awesome display of power, in a still small voice, or in the sound of complete silence. Let your Spirit flow within and among all of us, that our hearts may become yours and our minds may better understand your glory in this world. Amen.

Call to Confession
As a body, we turn our hearts to a time of confession before our God. God has promised that those who turn in humility to God, confessing their sins and asking for forgiveness will receive their pardon through the Lord, Jesus the Christ. Let us confess together our sinfulness.

Prayer of Confession
Holy God, we confess that we have not loved you as we ought. We have chased after idols instead of following you, the living God. We confess that we have not loved our neighbors as you taught, but have followed after things that lift us up and comfort us alone. Help us to see the need in

your world, help us to faithfully respond to that need, and forgive our human desires to do anything other than your will.

Assurance of Forgiveness
We are no longer imprisoned by the law. Instead, we have been redeemed through our savior Jesus the Christ. What was once under law is now under grace. Righteousness, which was once unattainable for us, is now possible through the gift of the Christ. As we have confessed, we have been forgiven. Praise God!

Offertory Invitation
We have come professing our faith in the God of our ancestors. There is none like God. As we give of our many blessings, we remember the source of all blessings, and the needs of many in this area and around the world. Let us give faithfully and generously.

Offertory Prayer
LORD, please accept the offerings we give to you this day. May they be faithful expressions of the gratitude we have for your many gifts to us. Please help us to use them for your purposes in this world. May they heal, feed, and carry your word to the ends of the earth. Amen.

Benediction
God has spoken to us this day, whether in grand gestures or in stillness and silence.
Receive God's blessings. May God go with you, may God sustain you, and may God grant that you can give of yourself to show God's love to others.
Amen.

Proper 8

Scripture
2 Kings 2:1-2, 6-14 or 1 Kings 19:15-16, 19-21
Psalm 77:1-2, 11-20 or Psalm 16
Galatians 5:1, 13-25
Luke 9:51-62

Call to Worship
One: I cry aloud to God;
Aloud to God that God might hear me.
Many: In the day of trouble I seek the LORD.
I will remember your wonders of old.
One: I will meditate on all your works,
I will think of your mighty deeds.
Many: Your way, O God, is holy.
What god is so great as our God?
One: You are the God who works wonders.
You have displayed your might among the people.
Many: Your way has always been to lead your people,
Yet your footsteps are unseen. Glory to you, O LORD!

Invocation
We have come here to meet you, the one true living God. We have come with excitement in our hearts, with praises on our lips, and with love in our hearts. Allow your people to have a double portion of your Spirit this day, just as Elisha requested so long ago. Move in us, break us, re-mold us, change us. Amen.

Call to Confession
The law is summed up in one single command, "You shall love your neighbor as yourself." How have we treated our neighbors? How have we treated our God? When we take the hard look at our lives that we must take, we will certainly see there are many ways we have sinned. Let us confess together.

Prayer of Confession
Wonderful Creator and Master of All, we confess that we have been drawn in by the promises of this world. We have used others as a means to get what we want. We have not acknowledged ways that our actions affect the poor and the abused of this world. We have not revered you as the master of our lives. Forgive these ways, O LORD, and renew in us the strength to love as you have taught.

Assurance of Forgiveness
Christ has already set us free. The work Christ did on our behalf has allowed us to have more than hope; it has allowed us to have faith that our sins are forgiven when we bring them before God and ask for God's forgiveness. We know that in Christ we are healed.

Offertory Invitation
We have all received of the fruits of the Spirit. Each of us has received some of these gifts. The time of offering is not simply a time to give money, it is a time to determine to give back to God out of all the gifts we have received. Let us worship God by giving of all we are.

Offertory Prayer
Great One, we lay our gifts before you. They are more than just our treasures, they are our very selves, all that we have and all we can do. We pray that you would use these gifts, that our outreach to your people may be stronger, our love may be more evident, and your kingdom on earth would grow. Amen.

Benediction
Let us say to our master,
"We will follow you wherever you go..."
Let us live this statement in all our days.
And may the Creator, the Savior, and the Holy Spirit bless us as we determine to follow the Christ.
Amen.

Proper 9

Scripture
2 Kings 5:1-14 or Isaiah 66:10-14
Psalm 30 or Psalm 66:1-9
Galatians 6:(1-6), 7-16
Luke 10:1-11, 16-20

Call to Worship
One: I will extol you, O LORD!
I will praise you and never cease praising!
Many: For you have drawn me up.
You have not let my foes rejoice against me.
One: O LORD, you have restored me to life.
Let us all give thanks to God's holy name!
Many: God's anger is but a moment; but God's favor lasts a lifetime.
Weeping may linger for the night, but joy comes in the morning.
One: Hear our cries once again, O LORD.
Hear and be gracious unto us.
Many: You have turned our mourning into dancing.
Therefore, we will praise you and never be silent.

Invocation
We lift our praises to you, Mighty and Awesome God. You are all power, all love, all blessing to us and to the world in which we live. We look to you and we greet you here. Fill our hearts and minds with such love, such peace, such desire to do your will that we can do nothing else. Amen.

Call to Confession
The history of God's people is a guide. When the people have humbled themselves before God, confessing their sins and working to be better people, God has forgiven those sins and has offered redemption. As we confess our sins to God this day, we join with the many generations who have gratefully received forgiveness from the God of all times.

Prayer of Confession
O God forgive our sinfulness. We are a people who have been far from you. We have not followed your way. We have chased after idols, things of the earth that we have substituted for you in our lives. We are sorry for all the ways we have sinned against you, and we ask for your forgiveness.

Assurance of Forgiveness
The prophet Isaiah wrote that as a mother comforts her child, so will God comfort God's people. We are God's children, and in God's grace we who have confessed and repented of our sins are forgiven in the name of Jesus Christ. Thanks be to God!

Offertory Invitation
The gifts of God, given to each of us, are intended to be shared with all of us. We are encouraged to offer the gifts God has given, different gifts for each one of us, for the good of the worshiping community. We offer our gifts of money and our other sacrificial gifts during these moments of worship.

Offertory Prayer
LORD, bless these gifts. Make them greater than they could ever be without you. Help them to make a real difference in this world, in our lives, and in the lives of all your people. We ask this in Jesus' holy name. Amen.

Benediction
The harvest is plentiful, but the laborers are few.
Let us go with the blessing of our Lord, Jesus the Christ,
to labor in God's vineyard.
Receive the blessings of our God,
The blessed Trinity, now and forever more.
Amen.

Proper 10

Scripture
Amos 7:7-17 *or Deuteronomy 30:9-14*
Psalm 82 *or Psalm 25:1-10*
Colossians 1:1-14
Luke 10:25-37

Call to Worship
One: God reigns above the cosmos,
God judges the world and all that is in it.
Many: O God, show your mercy to your servants.
Judge us with grace, show your compassion to your people.
One: Give justice to the weak and the orphan, O God.
Maintain the right of the lowly and destitute.
Many: Rescue the weak and needy.
Deliver them from the hand of the wicked.
One: Rise up, O God, and show your greatness.
Rescue those in need and give your gifts of mercy to those in trouble.
Many: God, you alone reign above the cosmos.
Glory to you, and to you alone!

Invocation
LORD, you have been our keeper and our salvation from the earliest of days. You have formed us, and you know us. We call upon you this day to renew the covenant within us. Make us like you. Make us like Jesus the Christ. Fill us with your Holy Spirit that we may worship you truly and come to know you more deeply in this time of worship. Amen.

Call to Confession
The LORD spoke through the prophet Amos that God was going to set a plumb line among the people of Israel. We are God's people, and we must examine ourselves to see if we would withstand such a plumb line of righteousness in this day. None are perfect. Let us confess together.

Prayer of Confession
God of all, we confess that we have been an imperfect people. We have tried, but we have still been sinful. In our thoughts, in our words, in our actions, and in those things, we have left unsaid or undone, LORD, we have sinned against you and your people. Please forgive us and cause us to be your faithful people.

Assurance of Forgiveness
The work has been done, the love of God has won the day. In the work of Christ, we have been redeemed. Because of the grace God has offered, all those who need forgiveness find it when we confess. Let us respond with great joy and thankfulness for this wonderful Assurance of Forgiveness.

Offertory Invitation
We are invited to give to God out of the gifts which God has given us. God has asked for our first and best, the first fruits of our labors and our harvests. Let us give generously, that the world may be blessed through what is received in this place.

Offertory Prayer
LORD, you have called us from earliest days to give of our gifts to you. May these gifts be acceptable to you, and may they be used so that people throughout this world, all our neighbors, might experience you love through the love of this body of Christ. Amen.

Benediction
The man who cared for the stranger on the road was a true neighbor to him.
Jesus proclaimed that his followers should go and do likewise.
Let us remember all people are our neighbors,
and let us do all we can to care for their needs.
Amen.

Proper 11

Scripture
Amos 8:1-12 *or Genesis 18:1-10a*
Psalm 52 *or Psalm 15*
Colossians 1:15-28
Luke 10:38-42

Call to Worship
One: The LORD honors those who do not boast,
Those who do not rejoice in the mischief done against the godly.
Many: Those who plot destruction all day long, who work treachery,
Those are not living according to God's way.
One: The righteous live according to the words of our God.
They rejoice in good and despise evil.
Many: Those who place their trust in riches and earthly wealth,
They will be utterly disappointed.
One: Instead, God's righteous are like green olive trees in the house of God.
They trust in the steadfast love of God forever and ever.
Many: Let us give thanks to God forever, because of what God has done.
In the presence of the faithful, we will proclaim God's name, for it is good.

Invocation
Holy God, your word is true, and your promises are sure. You have promised to meet with us whenever we are together in worship of you. Fulfill that promise today in great and powerful ways. Enter into us again, filling us with your spirit of goodness. Make us to be yours and only yours this day and every day. Amen.

Call to Confession
All people in the world live at times in a way that Paul describes as "estranged and hostile in mind, doing evil deeds." It is through the love and grace of Jesus the Christ that we become reconciled to God. As a body we confess our sins to God, that we may be forgiven for all our misdeeds.

Prayer of Confession
LORD God, you are merciful and kind. You call us to confession, asking us to repent of the ways that we have not lived up to our calling as your children. Please show us where we have fallen short, and give us hearts of true repentance, that we may be made clean and live acceptably before you.

Assurance of Forgiveness
God was pleased to reconcile all things to Godself through Jesus, the Christ and Savior of the world. We who are in Christ are forgiven whenever we come before God, repenting of our sinful ways. God is completely and forever faithful to reconcile those who recognize their sins. You are forgiven! Let us rejoice before our loving and gracious God!

Offertory Invitation
One calling of the people of God is to give to the community, that the outreach of the gathered faithful may be a force for love and health for people the world over. Let us faithfully examine our means and give as we are able that the blessings of God may extend far beyond our walls.

Offertory Prayer
God, you have given all gifts, and our first response should always be one of thankfulness for our blessings. We also are thankful for the opportunity to give and help make your way and your love known throughout the world. Please use these gifts to accomplish your desires wherever and in whatever way you choose. Amen.

Benediction
There is need of only one thing;
Total focus on the Lord, Jesus, the Christ.
May the Lord Jesus bless you and keep you,
In all your days and in every way.
Amen.

Proper 12

Scripture
Hosea 1:2-10 *or Genesis 18:20-32*
Psalm 85 *or Psalm 138*
Colossians 2:6-15, (16-19)
Luke 11:1-13

Call to Worship
One: LORD, you were favorable to your land;
You restored the fortunes of Jacob.
Many: You forgave the iniquity of your people;
You pardoned all their sins.
One: Restore us again, O God of our salvation.
Speak peace to your people, to those who turn to you in our hearts.
Many: Surely God's salvation is at hand for those who fear God.
May your glory, O LORD, dwell in our land.
One: Faithfulness will spring up from the ground,
And righteousness will look down from the sky.
Many: The LORD will give what is good, and our land will yield increase.
Righteousness will go before God and will make a path for all God's steps.

Invocation
LORD God, your promises are sure and your love for us is steadfast. We have gathered together to worship you, and you alone. We pray that all the elements of our worship service would bring you glory. Let us hear your voice and praise your name in our music, in our prayers, in our reading of Scripture, in our silences, and in every other way we worship you this day. Amen.

Call to Confession
Our need for forgiveness is ever before us. As followers of Christ, we realize that our forgiveness comes through Jesus' atonement for us. Jesus has commanded us to repent of our sins, that we may be healed. We need to recognize our sins before God and pray for forgiveness.

Prayer of Confession
Gracious God, and great healer of the universe, we confess that we have sinned in our lives against you and against your people. We have not only sinned in our individual lives, we have participated in ways that the culture of the world has created priority of some people over others and forgotten about those who have little power or agency. Please help us to recognize our sins, and work to heal ourselves and our communities.

Assurance of Forgiveness
God is holy and in God there can be no unholiness. Without the forgiveness that God has given through our Savior, we would have no hope of salvation. Thanks to God that because of Jesus' work we are forgiven in Jesus' name when we confess and repent! Believers, when you have confessed, you have been forgiven!

Offertory Invitation
We are tempted to follow after other wants and desires in our lives than those of our God. But God has commanded, and we have promised, that our first concern will be for God and God's work in the world. Let us give our best and first fruits that God's work may be done in the world.

Offertory Prayer
LORD, may these gifts become offerings that will join with many other offerings the world over to work toward the healing of creation. May we be ever grateful givers, and may we dedicate all we have and all we can be to caring for your people in the world. Amen.

Benediction
The fullness of deity dwells in Jesus Christ our Lord.
We have come to our fullness in Christ, the head of all rulers and authorities.
May God bless all of us that our fullness may shine before all,
and that we may shine Christ's love wherever we are found.
Amen.

Proper 13

Scripture
Hosea 11:1-11 *or Ecclesiastes 1:2, 12-14, 2:18-23*
Psalm 107:1-9, 43 *or Psalm 49: 1-12*
Colossians 3:1-11
Luke 12:13-21

Call to Worship
One: O give thanks to the LORD, for God is good!
God's steadfast love endures forever!
Many: Let the redeemed of the LORD say so, those redeemed from trouble
Those gathered in from the lands, from the east and west, north and south.
One: Some wandered in desert wastes, finding no way to an inhabited town.
Hungry and thirsty, their souls fainted within them.
Many: Then they cried to the LORD in their trouble,
And God delivered them from their distress.
One: Let them thank the LORD for God's steadfast love
And for God's wonderful works to humankind.
Many: For God satisfies the thirsty, and the hungry are filled with good things.
Let those who are wise remember and consider the steadfast love of the LORD.

Invocation
O LORD, you are good and your love for your people is grace-filled and everlasting. We have known your presence in our times of worship, devotion, prayer, and silence. Visit us again this day. Blow the winds of your spirit through this sanctuary again, renewing us with the intensity of your love. Amen.

Call to Confession
God says that the more God called the children of Israel, the more they went away from God. The people were unfaithful then, and they are unfaithful now. Let us turn our thoughts to ourselves and our unfaithfulness to God's ways and let us ask together for forgiveness.

Prayer of Confession
LORD of all, you are great in mercy. When we are honest, we know that it is your mercy that we need most of all. Please forgive the ways we have lost sight of your commands in our lives. Help us to see what we have done that is against your will and help us to have true hearts of repentance.

Assurance of Forgiveness
Faith in Christ has set us free from the burdens of sin. While we are still imperfect, we have the assurance that when we confess our sins to God, the grace of Christ will cover them. Give thanks to the LORD, because you are forgiven!

Offertory Invitation
God has called us to give for the glory of God, the good of the community, and the healing of the world. We are not intended to simply build bigger barns to keep all our things. Instead, we are called to give so that others may have what they need. Let us worship God through those gifts.

Offertory Prayer
LORD, you are good, and your mercy endures forever. Our gifts could never be enough to thank you for the blessings you have given to us, your people. Please accept these gifts that they may bring healing to your world and glory to your name. Amen.

Benediction
As you leave this day,
Be renewed in mind, body, and spirit,
Receiving the love of Christ our Savior,
To whom is all glory, honor, and power.
Amen.

Proper 14

Scripture
Isaiah 1:1, 10-20 *or Genesis 15:1-6*
Psalm 50:1-8, 22-23 *or Psalm 33:12-22*
Hebrews 11:1-3, 8-16
Luke 12:32-40

Call to Worship
One: The mighty one, God the LORD, speaks
And summons the earth from the rising of the sun to its setting
Many: Our God comes and does not keep silence.
Before God is a devouring fire, and a mighty tempest is all around.
One: The heavens declare the righteousness of our God.
For God is the judge of all that was, is, and is to come.
Many: Hear, O people, and listen to the word of the LORD.
Bring your sacrifices to God, sacrifices of that which you have received.
One: The LORD calls together the faithful ones.
Those who have given themselves to the LORD, God calls into community.
Many: Those who bring thanksgiving and their sacrifices before the LORD,
To those, God has promised to show salvation.

Invocation
Thank you, God of all, for welcoming us into this sanctuary. This is your house, this is a place where we come to seek you and to learn of you and to learn of your Spirit. Help us to empty ourselves in these moments as we prepare for worship. Help us to empty ourselves so we can be more fully filled by you. Let us know, when we leave this place, that we have been with the master of the universe. Amen.

Call to Confession
By faith we enter into God's presence so that we may lay down our sins before God. We are aware of our imperfections. We have received the promise that, when we come before God and truly confess those sins, God will hear, and God will heal. With faithfulness, we confess together.

Prayer of Confession
Gracious One, we bow down before you, all too aware of the ways we have fallen short of being the people you have called us to be. We have forgotten our promises to you and have chased after the things of the

world instead. We have not loved others as we should, instead, we have viewed others as means to get those things we want. Forgive our sinful ways and remake us in your image.

Assurance of Forgiveness
The grace of the Lord Jesus Christ is sufficient to cover any sin we may have committed. As we turn to God in love, owning up to our misdeeds, and confessing them, and as we lay those deeds aside pushing toward the better way, God will be faithful to forgive. Thanks be to God for this awesome news!

Offertory Invitation
Jesus spoke to those around saying, "Sell your possessions and give alms. Make purses for yourselves that do not wear out, and unfailing treasure in heaven, where no thief comes, and no moth destroys. For where your treasure is, there will your heart be also." Let us give as Jesus has called.

Offertory Prayer
LORD, change our hearts into hearts of love for you and for your people. Take what we have set aside during this time of offering. Help all our offerings to reach into your world, showing your love to people near and far away. Amen.

Benediction
Faith is the assurance of the things for which we hope.
Faith is the conviction of things we have not seen.
Be strengthened in your faith by the love of God,
the grace of the Savior, and the inspiration of the Spirit.
Amen.

Proper 15

Scripture
Isaiah 5:1-7 *or Jeremiah 23:23-29*
Psalm 80:1-2, 8-19 *or Psalm 82*
Hebrews 11:29-12:2
Luke 12:49-56

Call to Worship
One: Give ear, O Shepherd of Israel, you who lead Joseph like a flock!
You who are enthroned upon the cherubim, shine forth!
Many: You brought your people as a vine out of Egypt.
You planted them in the land you chose for them.
One: You cleared the ground for your vine.
It took deep root and it filled the land.
Many: You cared for your people like a shepherd cares for a flock.
You tended your people as a gardener cares for the crops.
One: May we, your people in this day, never turn away from you.
Give us life and let us call upon your name.
Many: Restore us, O LORD God of hosts;
Let your face shine on us, that we may be saved.

Invocation
Your love led the Israelites out of Egypt. Your love led the nation out of captivity. Your love gave us salvation in the form of the Christ. Shine your love in this place, here and now. Reveal yourself to us and send us your word again. Blow into this place with the mighty wind of your Spirit and grant that we may be overcome by your glory.

Call to Confession
Every one of us, every human on the earth, should come to a time of confession in our lives. God knows our inner and outer imperfections. God knows we are not perfect creatures. And God calls us to confess so that we may be forgiven. Let all who desire forgiveness pray together.

Prayer of Confession
Holy One, you have called us to be different from the world, loving you, following you, and living in righteousness. We know we have failed in living the life you have asked us to live. We have sinned. We have broken faith with you and with one another. We are truly sorry for our choices, and we humbly ask that you would forgive us, heal us, and restore us.

Assurance of Forgiveness
By faith we have come to God and in humility asked God for forgiveness and healing. Through faith we know that God will forgive all we have done. The grace that is offered by our God is unlimited. Whatever we have done, when we confess, God's grace covers it all. Thanks be to the Gracious Creator of the cosmos!

Offertory Invitation
The call is repeated in **Scripture** time and time again. What we are able to give, we are commanded to give so that the needs of all people and the purposes of God can be fulfilled. When we give and work together, we can accomplish so much more! Let us give generously, just as we have been blessed generously.

Offertory Prayer
What we have laid before you, awesome God, could never repay your grace, you love, your mercy for humanity. It could never repay all you have given to just a single one of us. Nevertheless, we pray for your blessing so these offerings can be all they are intended to be. Let us show your love, your grace, and your mercy to our world, through loving acts of kindness to neighbors and deeds that glorify your name. Amen.

Benediction
May Jesus, the pioneer and perfecter of our faith,
Who is now seated at the right hand of God,
Give you all blessing and wisdom and strength
To serve God with all you have and all you are,
This day, and every day.
Amen.

Proper 16

Scripture
Jeremiah 1:4-10 *or Isaiah 58:9b-14*
Psalm 71:1-6 *or Psalm 103:1-8*
Hebrews 12:18-29
Luke 13:10-17

Call to Worship
One: In you, O LORD, I take refuge.
Never let me be put to shame.
Many: In your righteousness deliver me and rescue me.
Incline your ear to me and save me.
One: Be to me a rock of refuge, a strong fortress.
Save me, because you are my rock and fortress.
Many: Rescue me, O my God, from the hand of the wicked,
From the grasp of the unjust and cruel.
One: For you, O LORD, are my hope.
My trust, O LORD, from my youth.
Many: Upon you I have leaned from my birth, it was you who brought me to life.
My praise is continually of you.

Invocation
LORD, our God, you have brought us into life and you have formed our inmost parts. We owe our very existence to you. When you breathed life to us, you filled us with your breath. We have received the winds of your Holy Spirit. Breathe into us again and renew us. Make us new by the power of your Spirit. Send your Spirit into this place that we may be who you desire us to be. Amen.

Call to Confession
In our weakness, we have sinned. In this, we are no different than others the world over. All humanity sins. But we live the lives of the redeemed, and we have received the promise that, even though we sin, we are set free from sin through Christ our Lord when we confess and repent of those sins. Let us confess together.

Prayer of Confession
Gracious and loving God, we are painfully aware of ways that we have sinned against you and against your creation. We have hurt one another. We have chased after things that do not satisfy in the pursuit of fleeting

happiness. We have chosen ways that are against the ways you have taught. Forgive us, O Lord, and continue to set us apart for your service.

Assurance of Forgiveness
The LORD is merciful and gracious, slow to anger and quick to forgive. When God's people turn to God in repentance, God will faithfully forgive. Wherever we have been, whatever we have done, once we choose in our hearts to turn from those sinful ways and repent, God has already forgiven. Thanks be to God!

Offertory Invitation
As we come to our opportunity for offering, let us search our hearts. We are called to be cheerful givers. We are called to give compassionately. Let us give with great love for God and God's creation, in faith that the love of God may be spread throughout the world from this place. Come and give.

Offertory Prayer
The gifts that we collect now, O LORD, we dedicate to you. We pray for your blessings upon them, that they may become symbols to all of the love of God given to the world. May we always use our gifts to praise you and to glorify you in your world. Amen.

Benediction
Go now with the blessings of the Great Trinity,
Loving, serving, and caring for all you may encounter,
In the name of Christ Jesus our Lord.
Amen.

Proper 17

Scripture
Jeremiah 2:4-13 *or Proverbs 25:6-7*
Psalm 81:1, 10-16 *or Psalm 112*
Hebrews 13:1-8, 15-16
Luke 14:1, 7-14

Call to Worship
One: Sing aloud to God, our strength!
Shout for joy to the God of Jacob!
Many: The LORD is our God, who brought the people out of Egypt.
Our God is our helper and redeemer.
One: God continues to redeem the people,
God still leads us from bondage, our bondage to sin.
Many: God promises to feed the faithful with the finest of wheat,
And God provides honey from the rock to satisfy.
One: Walk closely with God and observe God's ways;
Follow the statutes of the LORD, our shepherd.
Many: Sing aloud to God, our strength!
Shout for joy to the God of Jacob!

Invocation
LORD, you have been our strength from all ages. You brought us to life and you sustain us in our lives. We bow before you this day. We are here to worship you, to meet with you, to come to know you better. Reveal yourself to us in new and powerful ways as we worship you in this time. Fill us with your Spirit that we may walk with you. Amen.

Call to Confession
The way of this world is a sinful way. Even those who strive to follow the pathways of the Godly will still find themselves to be sinful people. It is our privilege to come before God, confessing our sins, and anticipating God's forgiveness. Let us pray together.

Prayer of Confession
God of Grace, we are thankful for the opportunity to offer our heartfelt confessions to you. We are a sinful people. We have not followed you as we ought. We have not offered hospitality to all our sisters and brothers. Please forgive our sins and help us to repent in lasting truth.

Assurance of Forgiveness

We say with confidence that the Lord is our helper. We shall not be afraid. When we confess our sins to God and ask for God's forgiveness, God is faithful to wash our sins from us. We are made new and whole. People of God, in the name of Jesus Christ, your sins are forgiven.

Offertory Invitation
We offer our sacrifice of praise to God in this time of worship. We have an opportunity to sacrifice of many things in our lives at this time. God desires our sacrifices for the well-being of the world and for the proper centering of God in our own lives. Let us give generously, showing our love for God and God's people.

Offertory Prayer
As we bring our gifts to you this day, O LORD, we ask for your blessing. May these gifts become in your hands greater than they could ever be in our hands alone. Let them heal those who suffer, feed those who hunger, and help all who are in need. We dedicate ourselves to you. Amen.

Benediction
May God bless us all,
With mutual love and understanding,
With gifts for hospitality,
And with all gifts of the Spirit
That we may show love and grace and mercy to all we meet.
Amen.

Proper 18

Scripture
Jeremiah 18:1-11 *or Deuteronomy 30:15-20*
Psalm 139:1-6, 13-18 *or Psalm 1*
Philemon 1:1-21
Luke 14:25-33

Call to Worship
One: O LORD, you have searched us and known us.
You know when we sit down and when we rise up.
Many: You discern thoughts from far away.
You know the paths of all people, and their lying down.
One: You are acquainted with all our ways.
Even before a word is on our tongues, you know it completely.
Many: You hem us in, behind and before.
You lay your hand upon us.
One: Such knowledge is too wonderful for us;
It is so high, we cannot attain it.
Many: You knit us together and formed our inward parts.
We praise you, because we are fearfully and wonderfully made.

Invocation
LORD God, you have made your people, and you have made us a wonder. Each breath of life, each cell, each moment is a mystery to us, and yet you have given us life and sustained us and made us yours. Enter into us again this day, this hour, this moment. Renew our minds, bodies, and souls. Help us to see you and help us to be who you want us to be. Amen.

Call to Confession
The call of the gospel is expensive. It demands from us sometimes more than we feel able to give. Salvation comes through faith alone, but discipleship is costly. God expects us to live according to the word. Christ commands us to give up the things that we have in order to be disciples. Let us confess the ways we have not lived up to this calling.

Prayer of Confession
LORD God, Creator of us all, you have demanded of us that we will follow your footsteps in all our days. Jesus commanded us to love you before even our closest family. We have failed in these calls time and time again. Please forgive us. Please move in us to be different. Please cause us to take your calls seriously that we may try harder to live up to them.

Assurance of Forgiveness
The grace of Jesus the Christ is great, greater than all the sinfulness in the history of the world. God's demands on us are overwhelming, but thank God, God's mercy is also overwhelming. Through our heartfelt confessions we are healed. Thanks be to God!

Offertory Invitation
Jesus says that we must give away all, everything, in order to become Jesus' disciple. What are we willing to give? What are we unwilling to part with, so we can be Jesus' disciples? What might we be tempted to hold back? Let us examine our hearts and give accordingly.

Offertory Prayer
Holy One, please bless these gifts we give this day. We recognize that they do not fulfill Christ's call to give all of our possessions. Help us have the faith to give more. And help us to have the willingness that, even those things that are not offered in these moments, may be dedicated to you so that all we have and all we are may be used by you for your glory and for the benefit of your people. Amen.

Benediction
The gifts of God are many.
Go, sharing of the gifts you have received with all you meet,
And as you do, may God the Creator,
God the Savior,
and God the Holy Spirit bless you deeply and richly.
Amen.

Proper 19

Scripture
Jeremiah 4:11-12, 22-28 *or Exodus 32:7-14*
Psalm 14 *or Psalm 51:1-10*
1 Timothy 1:12-17
Luke 15:1-10

Call to Worship
One: Have mercy upon us, O God, according to your steadfast love.
According to your abundant mercy, blot out our transgressions.
Many: Wash us thoroughly from our iniquity.
Cleanse us from our sin.
One: You desire truth in our inward being,
Therefore, teach us wisdom in our secret hearts.
Many: Wash us thoroughly from our iniquity.
Cleanse us from our sin.
One: Let us hear joy and gladness.
Wash us, and we shall be whiter than snow.
Many: Wash us thoroughly from our iniquity.
Cleanse us from our sin.

Invocation
We come today proclaiming faith in you, O God. We trust in you, we place all our hopes in you, the master of the universe. Remove our doubts. Remove our reservations. Cause us to place ourselves completely in your hands and give ourselves completely to your providence. Meet us here and make us new once again. Amen.

Call to Confession
If we say we have no sin, we are deceiving ourselves. We are, just like the rest of humanity, sinners in need of God's mercy and salvation. Our opportunity for cleansing is repentance. Let us confess our sins before God, truly determining to turn from those sins, and let us ask for God's forgiveness.

Prayer of Confession
Holy and Loving God, we praise you because you have given us the chance to be made whole, even when we have fallen short of your plans for our lives. As we have done this, we have sinned, and we come before you, humbly recognizing those sins, and admitting that there are likely many others we have forgotten or not recognized. Please forgive them all and lead us in your truth.

Assurance of Forgiveness
Repenting of our sin is not an easy endeavor. It means feeling heartily sorry for our misdeeds, and then determining to avoid those deeds in the future. When we have examined ourselves, and when we have truly repented of our sins, God will always be faithful to forgive. Let us live our lives in truth for our God.

Offertory Invitation
What shall we return to God for all the blessings God has given to us? Jesus desires us to be willing to give all to care for all God's sheep, and to be true disciples of Christ. As we give, let us give our money, yes, but also our time, our skills, our selves that God may be glorified.

Offertory Prayer
We offer these gifts to you, loving God. We pray that they are the first and best fruits of which we have received. Please take them unto yourself, give wisdom to all who may have access to using them, and allow them to be blessings unto your people in the world. Amen.

Benediction
Now, as we depart,
Remember to go into the world seeking the lost.
And to the King of the ages,
Immortal, Invisible, the only God,
Be honor and glory forever and ever.
Amen.

Proper 20

Scripture
Jeremiah 8:18-9:1 *or Amos 8:4-7*
Psalm 79:1-9 *or Psalm 113*
1 Timothy 2:1-7
Luke 16:1-13

Call to Worship
One: Praise the LORD! Praise, O servants of the LORD.
Praise the Holy Name of our God!
Many: Blessed be the name of the LORD from this time on and forevermore.
From the rising of the sun to its setting the name of the LORD is to be praised.
One: The LORD is high above all nations,
God's glory is above the heavens.
Many: Who is like the LORD our God who is seated on high,
Who looks far down on the heavens and the earth?
One: God raises the poor from the dust.
God lifts the needy from the ash heap to make them sit with princes.
Many: God gives the barren a home,
Making them the joyous parents of children. Praise the LORD!

Invocation
LORD God, you brought this world out of nothing, and you continue to sustain and breathe life into our world. Grant that we may see you clearly in this time of worship. Blow with your winds of love into our worship space and into the hearts of all your people. As we recognize you, make us more like you, that we may not leave the same as we were when entered this place. Make us new. Make us yours. Amen.

Call to Confession
One of the greatest gifts given to us by our God is the opportunity to be made new and clean through our time of confession. We turn in this time to God, recognizing our sins, asking to be forgiven, and praying for the strength to turn from our sinful ways in the future. Let us join together.

Prayer of Confession
LORD of all nations and all worlds, we confess that we are sinful people. We have forgotten your commands in our lives. We have lived as if wealth and personal gratification were our gods, instead of the one true God who

demands mercy and justice for the poor. Forgive us, we pray. Bring us into alignment with your just and holy desires for this world and give us the ability to live in the way you have called us to live.

Assurance of Forgiveness
God knows we are imperfect people, and yet God loves and desires salvation for all of us. God asks that we confess our sins to God and work toward true repentance and justice. When we do this, God is faithful to forgive. People of God, for whatever you have lifted to God in repentance, you are forgiven.

Offertory Invitation
A servant cannot serve two masters. Either the servant will hate the one and love the other or be devoted to the one and despise the other. You cannot serve both God and money. Let us choose to serve God this day.

Offertory Prayer
Holy God, master of all things, we choose to serve you instead of money. Please take these gifts of our labor, gifts of our hands, gifts of our abilities, and use them for your benefit and for the benefit of people throughout the world. Let us work toward equity and justice for all people, and may all people be blessed through our efforts. Amen.

Benediction
May the blessings of the Lord, Jesus the Christ,
The great and awesome love of God,
And the empowering fire of the Holy Spirit,
Go with you now,
Blessing you and compelling you to care for all God's children.
Amen.

Proper 21

Scripture
Jeremiah 32:1-3a, 6-15 *or Amos 6:1a, 4-7*
Psalm 91:1-6, 14-16 *or Psalm 146*
1 Timothy 6:6-19
Luke 16:19-31

Call to Worship
One: You who live in the shelter of the Most High,
Who abide in the shadow of the Almighty,
Many: We will say to the LORD, "Our refuge and our fortress;
Our God, in whom we place our trust."
One: For God will deliver you from the snare of the fowler.
God will rescue you from deadly pestilence.
Many: God will cover the people with pinions, and under God's wings we will find refuge.
God's faithfulness is a shield and armor to God's people.
One: You will not fear the terror of the night, or the arrow that flies by day,
"Those who love me, I will deliver," says our God. "I will protect those who know my name."
Many: "When they call to me, I will answer them. I will be with them in trouble.
I will rescue and honor them. I will satisfy them and show them my salvation."

Invocation
LORD God, maker of all that is seen and all that is unseen, show us your salvation this day. Be with us as we come here to worship you. Move in us, overwhelm us, invigorate us with the blessings of your Spirit and the motivations of your heart. Be in us, that we might live to serve you. Amen.

Call to Confession
We are called to keep God's commandments without spot or blame until Christ comes. That is the call to the people of God, but we are imperfect at best in living up to this call. Let us come together as one body confessing the ways we have sinned before God.

Prayer of Confession
The call you have given to us, Holy God, is a call for righteousness. But we

have been pulled by our own human desires and by the workings of this world toward sins that we recognize and sins we may not even realize we have committed. Please forgive our sins. Please open our eyes to your continuing call on our lives. Give us hearts of disciples, and in your love, renew us.

Assurance of Forgiveness
God's grace is all sufficient for us. We who love God are called to recognize the ways that we have failed to live up to God's calling for us. And when we recognize these things, and humbly come to God, seeking forgiveness, God is faithful to forgive. Thanks be to God, the one and only master of all things!

Offertory Invitation
The love of money is the root of all evil. Money itself, however, can do great good in this world to care for those in need and to support efforts that bring people into relationship with our Lord, Jesus Christ. Let us set aside our love for money and give generously that many lives may be touched.

Offertory Prayer
LORD, hear our prayer over these offerings today. Forgive our desires to keep for ourselves all you have given to us. Give us hearts of generosity that we may use our gifts, these gathered before us this day, and every gift we have received, for the glory of your name and the building of your kingdom. Amen.

Benediction
May you find your home,
In the shelter of the Most High.
May you find rest and protection under God's wings.
May God lift you up,
So that even your foot may not be dashed against a stone.
Amen.

Proper 22

Scripture
Lamentations 1:1-6 *or Habakkuk 1:1-4; 2:1-4*
Lamentations 3:19-26 or Psalm 137 *or Psalm 37:1-9*
2 Timothy 1:1-14
Luke 17:5-10

Call to Worship
One: Call the faithfulness of the LORD to mind,
Have hope in God, all people!
Many: The steadfast love of the LORD never ceases;
God's mercies never come to an end.
One: They are new every morning!
Great is the faithfulness of the LORD God Almighty!
Many: "The LORD is our portion," say our souls.
"Therefore, we shall place our trust in God."
One: The LORD is good to those who wait for God;
The LORD will give good to the soul that seeks God.
Many: It is good that one should wait quietly for the salvation of the LORD.
The steadfast love of the LORD never ceases!

Invocation
LORD of all, Great God above all people and all things, Master of the universe, and great and powerful Lover of creation, your steadfast love endures forever. We are here to meet you. We are here to have a new and fresh encounter with you. Show us your mercy, show us your love, show us your power, show us your abundance of faithfulness. Renew in us the fire of conviction to serve you and to love each other. Amen.

Call to Confession
God's faithfulness to humanity is everlasting and always steadfast. Our faithfulness to God is not as constant. In this time of worship we have the privilege to approach God, to ask for forgiveness, and through the grace of Jesus Christ, when we have confessed, to be forgiven. Let us offer our repentance before our God.

Prayer of Confession
Holy and Awesome God, we confess that we have not been faithful to our promises to you or to your commands to us. Your commands to us have been to love you and to love one another. Although these rules seem

simple, we have not faithfully lived them out. We have valued ourselves more highly than others and we have placed things above you in our lives. Forgive us, we pray, and make us whole.

Assurance of Forgiveness
The love of God be with you, the grace of Christ surround you! The blessings of God are able to make even the vilest offenses right again. When we recognize our misdeeds, when we turn to God, humbly confessing of our sins, and when we determine to repent, God has promised forgiveness. Thanks to our Lord Jesus the Christ, we are forgiven!

Offertory Invitation
Our service, our selves, and all that we have we should dedicate to God. As we come to this time of offering in our worship service, let us turn our hearts and minds to what we can give so that God's word may be spread across the globe. There is nothing too great to offer to God.

Offertory Prayer
God, you are all power, all wisdom, all grace-- all of everything. There is nothing we can give to you that you do not already possess. Please bless our efforts to give of what we have back to you. Use these gifts and all our treasure and talents to share your love with the world. We offer our very selves to you. Amen.

Benediction
God did not give a spirit of cowardice,
Rather God gave a spirit of power and of love and of self-discipline.
Let us go into the world with a spirit of power,
Showing the love of God,
And with the discipline of servants of God,
Sharing the word with all we meet.
Amen.

Proper 23

Scripture
Jeremiah 29:1, 4-7 *or 2 Kings 5:1-3, 7-15c*
Psalm 66:1-12 *or Psalm 111*
2 Timothy 2:8-15
Luke 17:11-19

Call to Worship
One: Make a joyful noise to God, all the earth;
Sing to the glory of God's name; give to God glorious praise.
Many: Say to God, "How awesome are your deeds!
Because of your great power, your enemies cringe before you."
One: All the earth worships you; they sing praises to you.
They sing praises to your name. Selah.
Many: Come and see what God has done!
God is awesome in deeds among all mortals.
One: God turned the sea into dry land, and the people passed through the river on foot.
There we rejoiced in God whose eyes keep watch on the nations.
Many: Bless our God, O peoples, let the sound of God's praise be heard,
Who has kept us among the living and has not let our feet slip.

Invocation
We come to you, O LORD, and we present ourselves to you as living sacrifices for you. Draw us into your love this day. Fill us with your holy fire of the Spirit that we may be energized and excited to do your work in the world. Cause us to seek you and you alone and grant that we may ever find you. Amen.

Call to Confession
In faith we offer our confessions to God, so that through faith God may forgive our sins. We recognize that we are imperfect creatures and that we deserve judgment for the ways we have sinned. We believe that God in perfect grace will forgive when we confess and repent. Let us join in prayer.

Prayer of Confession
Loving God, we confess that we have neglected you and your commands to us. We have participated in ways that marginalize others. We have feared and ostracized those who are different from us. For these and many other misdeeds, we confess, we have sorrow, and we ask that we may be forgiven. In your grace, hear our prayer, O God.

Assurance of Forgiveness
When we respond to God in faithfulness, remembering our sins and owning them, and then asking God for forgiveness, the faithfulness of God through our Lord Jesus will grant us redemption. We have confessed and repented together. As we have done so, we are forgiven. Thanks be to God!

Offertory Invitation
We are called to dedicate all we have to the glory of God and to the care of God's creation. We cannot show our love for God and for others while we hoard things for ourselves. Let us return to God our gifts for the glory of God and the good of our world.

Offertory Prayer
Hear our prayers, God of all, as we bring our first fruits to you. Bless this offering and bless us as givers. May these gifts be dedicated solely to you that you may be glorified and that all creation may be blessed through this congregation. We pray this in Jesus' name. Amen.

Benediction
If we have died with Christ, we will also live with Christ;
If we endure, we will also reign with Christ.
Let us go, proclaiming Christ,
And receiving blessings for our faithfulness to our Lord and Savior.
Amen.

Proper 24

Scripture
Jeremiah 31:27-34 *or Genesis 32:22-31*
Psalm 119:97-104 *or Psalm 121*
2 Timothy 3:14-4:5
Luke 18:1-8

Call to Worship
One: Oh, how your people love your law!
It is the meditation of our hearts all day long.
Many: Your commandments enlighten those who study them.
They make your followers wise beyond the world.
One: Those who follow your teaching are wiser than the aged.
They will hold their way back from evil, in order to keep your word.
Many: Those you have taught will not turn back from your ordinances.
Your teachings are written on their hearts.
One: How sweet are your words to your people!
They are sweeter than honey to the mouths of the faithful.
Many: Through your precepts your people gain understanding.
Therefore, they hate every false way.

Invocation
Your love and care for us, O LORD, is overwhelming. You teach us how to be your faithful people, writing your words on our hearts. Continue to teach us this day. Fill us with your Spirit that we may be refreshed in knowledge of you. Renew our hearts and minds and make us wholly yours now and throughout our lives. Amen.

Call to Confession
All our misdeeds, all our judgment of others, all our selfish desires are known to God. As imperfect as we are, we can be made whole by God when we bring our sins to God and confess them, repenting and humbly asking for God's mercy. Let us pray together.

Prayer of Confession
Forgive us, O God, we pray. We have been sinful people. We have neglected you and your word to us. We have been influenced by a world that values money over people, possessions over relationships, and many false gods over you, the one true God. Forgive us, we pray, and lead us forward in righteousness.

Assurance of Forgiveness
God offers forgiveness to all those who ask, when they come to God with repentance in their hearts and when they turn from their sinful ways. We, who have recognized our sin before God this day, have confessed those sins, and have prayed for strength to avoid sin in the future, are forgiven by a loving God and through the gift of our Savior. Glory to the Triune God!

Offertory Invitation
We are exhorted to continue the work that was begun in Christ Jesus in our world. Although it is many years later, there is a great need for workers to spread the message of the Christ. One way we do this as a community is by combining our resources in order to support missionaries who carry God's message to the world, our local church that proclaims the message in this place, and the global church that continues to seek salvation for all. Let us give generously.

Offertory Prayer
We lay our treasures before you, loving God, and we humbly request your blessing. Please bless all the offerings we have to give, so that they may be used to show love to your people and share the good news of salvation to a needy world. We pray for blessings of strength, of sureness of purpose, and of boldness in leading others to the loving Christ. May these gifts be used for your purposes. Amen.

Benediction
With God's blessing,
Continue in what you have learned,
And what we firmly believe,
Knowing from whom you have learned it.
And may God our great Creator,
Jesus Christ, God's Son and our Savior,
And the empowering Holy Spirit,
Be with us all as we serve the Trinity.
Amen.

Proper 25

Scripture
Joel 2:23-32 *or Jeremiah 14:7-10, 19-22*
Psalm 65 *or Psalm 84:1-7*
2 Timothy 4:6-8, 16-18
Luke 18:9-14

Call to Worship
One: Praise is due to you, O God, of all the earth.
To you shall our vows be made and performed.
Many: We call to you, the one who answers prayer!
To you all flesh shall come in fullness of time.
One: When deeds of iniquity overwhelm us, you forgive our transgressions.
Happy are those who live near to your courts.
Many: We shall be satisfied with the goodness of your house;
With the wonders of your holy temple.
One: By awesome deeds you answer us with deliverance,
O God of our salvation. You are the hope of all.
Many: All creation sings together of your awe and majesty.
You are girded with might.

Invocation
O LORD, our God, you are indeed holy, and the only one who is truly righteous. We are happy to be found in your temple, because we know when we seek you we will always find you. Help us to know you better. Show us your paths for us as individuals and as communities. Give us the will and strength to follow those paths and help us to always continue to seek you. Amen.

Call to Confession
Our iniquities testify against us. These words from the prophet Jeremiah remind us that although we may even sometimes successfully hide our sinfulness from one another, it is always clear to God. We are called to confess our sins before God that we may receive forgiveness.

Prayer of Confession
Ancient and Holy God, we confess that our greed and desire have separated us from living justly in your world. We have craved things for ourselves and have sought them at the expense of others, of creation, and of our relationship to you. Please forgive us and help us to be the people you have called us to be.

Assurance of Forgiveness
The grace of the Lord Jesus Christ surrounds us and uplifts us when we humble ourselves and pray to God for forgiveness. Because God is loving, God has given us the opportunity to be made whole. When we confess and when we repent, we are made clean once again. People of God, we are forgiven.

Offertory Invitation
Give to the Most High as God has given to you, and as generously as you can afford. These words are echoed throughout **Scripture**. We are to give because it is an act of faithfulness. We are to give because others have need. We are to give because we must learn to deny ourselves. Let us give all we can.

Offertory Prayer
Creator and Master, we pray that you would receive these offerings given to you faithfully by your people. These gifts are a portion of what we offer to you. We also offer at this time our minds, our bodies, and our spirits. Use all our gifts that your world may become more like the kingdom you desire. Amen.

Benediction
Receive the blessings of the great God of all,
Creator, Savior, and Holy Spirit,
And go in the knowledge of these blessings,
Sharing the good news with all you meet.
Amen.

Proper 26

Scripture
Habakkuk 1:1-4; 2:1-4 *or Isaiah 1:10-18*
Psalm 119:137-144 *or Psalm 32:1-7*
2 Thessalonians 1:1-4; 11-12
Luke 19:1-10

Call to Worship
One: You are righteous, O LORD,
And your judgments are right.
Many: You have appointed your decrees in righteousness,
Your laws have been fashioned in all faithfulness.
One: Our zeal for you consumes us,
Help all your servants to remember your words.
Many: Your promises are well tried,
And your servants love them.
One: Though we are small and little to be regarded by you,
We will not forget your precepts.
Many: Your righteousness is an everlasting righteousness,
Give us understanding that we may receive your salvation.

Invocation
Holy God, we have gathered here to bring our sacrifice of worship to you. We praise you for the way you have made us, your people, and we are grateful that we have been called to this place to lift our voices together in worship. Meet us here and fill us with your love. Help us to come to know you better by our time with you and by revealing your heart to us. We love you, O LORD! Amen.

Call to Confession
Whatever we have been and done, wherever we have gone, God has salvation in store for us. We have a responsibility to do our best to live in the way God has called us to live. God promises to forgive us for our missteps when we confess and repent. Let us bow together in prayer before God.

Prayer of Confession
Holy and loving God, we confess that we have not been the people you have called us to be. We have gone our own way. We have loved ourselves more than others. We have sought after things that cannot truly satisfy. We set aside these sins, and we repent of them. Help us to live in your light.

Assurance of Forgiveness
Salvation has come to this place today! When we let go of our sinful ways, when we ask for forgiveness, and when we give ourselves back over to God, God will be faithful to forgive. In the name of Jesus the Christ, we are forgiven! Thanks be to the God of grace!

Offertory Invitation
It is our duty to give to the needs of God and of God's people. We are called to do just that during these moments of worship. Let us place the needs of God above our human wants and desires and let us give to God from our very hearts.

Offertory Prayer
LORD God, creator of the heavens and the earth, you have made all the things we have ever received. We offer these gifts to you, praying that you would bless them, that you would use them, and that you would give us your wisdom to use all our gifts in ways that glorify you and serve your creation. We pray all this in Christ's name. Amen.

Benediction
Grace to you, and peace,
From God our Creator and the Lord Jesus Christ.
May your love for one another increase abundantly,
And may your faith grow continually.
May these and many blessings be yours in Christ Jesus.
Amen.

Proper 27

Scripture
Haggai 1:15b-2:9 *or Job 19 23-27a*
Psalm 145:1-5, 17-21 *or Psalm 98 or Psalm 17:1-9*
2 Thessalonians 2:1-5, 13-17
Luke 20:27-38

Call to Worship
One: We will extol you, our God and King.
We will bless your name forever and ever.
Many: Every day we will bless you,
And we will sing praises to your name in all our days.
One: Great is the LORD, and greatly to be praised!
God's greatness is unsearchable.
Many: One generation shall laud your works to another.
We shall continually declare your mighty acts.
One: On the glorious splendor of your majesty,
And on all your wondrous works, we will meditate.
Many: Our mouths will speak the praise of the LORD,
And all flesh will bless God's holy name forever and ever.

Invocation
God of all, Maker of the universe, creator of the greatest galaxies and the tiniest particles, we rejoice that you are the God of the living. We invoke your name and presence in this place. Come, enter us. Come, commune with us. Come, inspire us to be your people, just as you are our God. We pray these things in the name of Christ our Lord. Amen.

Call to Confession
We are invited to examine ourselves and see the places where we have sinned against God and against God's creation. This is a task that should be difficult, because it reminds us of the things we have done against God's will. Let us call those things to mind now and ask for God's forgiveness.

Prayer of Confession
Gracious God, we humble ourselves before you, sorry for the ways that we have wandered from your path. We have sinned against you and we have hurt others. We turn to you, with hearts of repentance, and ask that you would accept us and forgive us.

Assurance of Forgiveness
We know that our redeemer lives, and that God is the one who redeems. God forgives a multitude of sins when we come to God, confessing our sinful nature, and asking God for forgiveness and renewal. We have confessed this day. We have declared our intention to repent. People of God, we are forgiven!

Offertory Invitation
At this time, we turn our hearts to worship of God in a special way. We take time to give of all we have received in order that God may be praised on earth and that God's message may be known throughout the globe. Let us give joyfully, in prayerful and praiseful worship.

Offertory Prayer
God and master of all, we bring these gifts to you for your blessing. We dedicate them entirely to your use in our church, in our community, and throughout the entire world. May we bless this world through the gifts that we have been given, and may we ever be found faithful in returning those gifts to you. Amen.

Benediction
Now may our Lord Jesus Christ,
And God our great Creator,
Who loved us and through grace gave us eternal comfort and good hope,
Comfort your hearts and strengthen them in every good work and word.
Amen.

Proper 28

Scripture
Isaiah 65:17-25 *or Malachi 4:1-2a*
Isaiah 12 *or Psalm 98*
2 Thessalonians 3:6-13
Luke 21:5-19

Call to Worship
One: We give thanks to you, O LORD,
We thank you for your comfort and for the grace you have shown to us.
Many: Surely God is our salvation; we will trust and not be afraid.
The LORD God is our strength and our might.
One: With joy we will draw from the water of the wells of salvation,
Because God has become our salvation.
Many: And in that day we will say:
Give thanks to the LORD; call upon God's name.
One: Make God's deeds known throughout the nations.
Proclaim them and exalt God's name.
Many: Sing praises to the LORD, for God has done gloriously.
Let this be known in all the earth.

Invocation
Source of all being, we come to you this day declaring our love, our dependence upon you, and our desire to learn of you. Hear our prayer from your sanctuary. Meet us. Fill us with your Spirit. Claim us as your own. Help us to encounter you this day that we may be your people in our hearts, minds, and spirits. Amen.

Call to Confession
It is our joy to have an advocate in Christ. We are aware that we are sinful people and in need of redemption. We have the opportunity in these moments to humbly confess our sins to God and ask for God's forgiveness. Let us pray together.

Prayer of Confession
LORD God, we have claimed to be your people, but we have not devoted our whole selves to you. We have allowed ourselves to be led astray by the world, by other people, and by the riches and pleasures to be found in our lives. Please forgive us. Renew our dedication to you. Renew our hearts and make them like yours.

Assurance of Forgiveness
God is faithful and will completely forgive all those who come to God in repentance and ask for God's pardon. We have confessed our sins this day. We have asked for the ability to truly repent, and we have asked all these things in the name of the Savior. In God's great grace, we are forgiven.

Offertory Invitation
God loves to witness God's people giving cheerfully. We have an opportunity in this time to give to God out of the gifts we have received, as an act of joyful worship. Let us give all we can with glad hearts to the work God is doing in our world.

Offertory Prayer
We offer these gifts to you, great God of all the universe. In comparison to all you have made, these gifts are very small. Yet we know as your followers that you can make much out of very little. Please bless these gifts that they may become great for you and for your people on earth. Amen.

Benediction
As sisters and brothers in Christ,
Let us work together to the glory of God,
And never tire.
And may the great God of all,
The Holy Trinity, three-in-one,
Bless us to do God's work in our world,
This day and every day.
Amen.

Proper 29 Reign of Christ

Scripture
Jeremiah 23:1-6
Luke 1:68-79 *or Psalm 46*
Colossians 1:11-20
Luke 23:33-43

Call to Worship
One: Blessed be the LORD God of Israel,
For God has looked favorably upon the people and redeemed them.
Many: God has raised up a mighty savior for us in the house of David,
Just as God spoke through the mouth of the holy prophets of old.
One: We are now saved from our enemies and the hand of all who hate us.
God has shown the mercy promised to our ancestors, remembering the holy covenant.
Many: The covenant was given to Abraham, that we might serve the LORD without fear.
We may serve in holiness and righteousness before God all our days.
One: The Christ gives knowledge of salvation to God's people by forgiveness of sins.
Jesus prepares the way of the LORD into this world.
Many: By the tender mercy of our God, the dawn from on high will break upon us,
To give light to those in darkness and to guide our feet into the way of peace.

Invocation
Living and loving God, we worship your majesty this day. You have brought into our world the very Christ, the ruler from time immemorial, to rule our hearts, and for those with eyes to see, to rule the very world. Illuminate us today. Teach us of you and of the Christ. Give us the wisdom of the Holy Spirit to guide our minds and thoughts and to teach us just who you are. Amen.

Call to Confession
We are called to come before our Great and Mighty God, through the love of the Christ, and offer our repentance for the misdeeds we have committed in our lives. All humanity stands in need of redemption, and through the grace of God, when we confess, we can be forgiven. Let us pray.

Prayer of Confession
Holy and gracious God, we praise you for your grace to us. We turn to you now in supplication, asking for your forgiveness. We know we have sinned. We have not been your people. We have fallen away from your calling for us. We have objectified others and we have not honored you properly. Please forgive our sins, God, and help us to become better followers of your way.

Assurance of Forgiveness
The grace of God and the love of the Christ be with you all! God is graceful indeed and has offered forgiveness to us when we are willing to humbly bow before God and confess our sins. In Christ we have redemption, the forgiveness of sins. For all we have confessed this day, we have been forgiven. Praise be to our gracious God!

Offertory Invitation
We observe this day in the church year as a special day to acknowledge Jesus the Christ as the ruler of the universe. There is nothing we have that we have not received from the master of all things. During this special time in our worship, we have the opportunity to give God glory through our giving to God. Let us make the most of this opportunity, giving sacrificially to praise Christ our Lord.

Offertory Prayer
God of all, receive our gifts, we pray, that your name may be known throughout the globe and that your love may be spread to all. In your hands these gifts can become powerful enough to bring about changes in our world. We pray that you may add your blessings to all these gifts, whether they are in our offering plates or in our hearts and grant that they may reach to your people wherever they are in need. Amen.

Benediction
We give thanks to God,
The Great Trinity,
And the Holy Ruler of all things,
And may we receive God's blessings as we leave this place.
Go now, giving love and sharing the grace
Of Christ, the ruler of all.
Amen.

All Saints Day

Scripture
Daniel 7:1-3, 15-18
Psalm 149
Ephesians 1:11-23
Luke 6:20-31

Call to Worship
One: Praise the LORD! Sing to the LORD a new song!
Sing God's praise in the assembly of the faithful!
Many: Let all the earth be glad in its maker.
Let the children of God rejoice in their King!
One: Let them praise God's name with dancing,
Making melody to God with tambourine and lyre.
Many: For the LORD takes pleasure in God's people.
God adorns the humble with victory.
One: Let the faithful exult in glory;
Let them sing aloud to God for joy.
Many: Let the high praises of God be in their throats.
Let them proclaim the glory of our God. Praise the LORD!

Invocation
We praise you God, because you are the eternal one. You call things into being out of nothing. You redeem your creation. We praise you for those who have walked your path before us, those who have run their race and fought the good fight. We pray for the goodness of all people everywhere and for the soon to come communion with you and all creation in the redeemed world. Amen.

Call to Confession
God calls us to a time of confession. It is a sacred opportunity to unburden ourselves of the things we have done that have separated us from obedience to God in our lives. Let us call to mind our sinful ways and let us offer our repentance before a gracious God.

Prayer of Confession
LORD, hear our prayer. We are your servants, but we have not served you in all goodness or with all our hearts. We have allowed other concerns to get in our way of devotion to you. We have not followed your rule to do unto others as we would have them do unto us. Forgive us, we pray.

Assurance of Forgiveness
God's power to redeem was made manifest in the resurrection of Christ our Lord. Through Christ's resurrection, the victory over death is complete. Through Christ's atonement, we can have the same victory over sin, when we are willing to confess. Redemption is ours in our Lord, Jesus Christ!

Offertory Invitation
The gifts of the saints throughout the years have brought us to this place. A great blessing for us is to be able to give to the church and to its ministries that we may sustain the worshiping community into new generations. Let us give, in love, that the world may know God's good news.

Offertory Prayer
Giving and loving God, we bring our sacrifices to you, offering them for your use and for the uplifting of your kingdom here on earth. We thank you for gifts that have sustained us in the past and we pray that all we offer here may be used to glorify you and to empower your Church for its work in the world. Amen.

Benediction
May the God of our Lord Jesus Christ give you a spirit of wisdom and revelation,
As you come to know God,
So that, with the eyes of your hearts enlightened,
You may know the hope to which God has called you,
The riches of God's glorious inheritance among the saints,
And the immeasurable greatness of God's power.
Amen.

www.ingramcontent.com/pod-product-compliance
Lightning Source LLC
Chambersburg PA
CBHW072050290426
44110CB00014B/1625